My Amish Life:

Leaving Family, Friends, And the Life I Knew

By Rebecca Miller

ISBN-10: 1984013920
ISBN-13: 978-1984013927

Printed in the United States of America

Cover design by iCreate Designs
Front cover photo is of Martha Beougher and Billy.
Back cover photo by Amanda Strater

CONTENTS

Acknowledgments

Thanks and appreciation to my husband who gave me extra quiet time and space as I typed day after day. Also, thanks to my son, Norman, whose patience was tried with my ignorance of the computer. With his knowledge and skill, I gained hope of the possibility of seeing my book completed.

During the writing of my book, I felt God leading me to the right people to help me find a way to complete the task before me, which at times felt like an impossibility.

Thanks for the support of my friend Linda Coulson who helped me with the first editing and who spoke kind words of encouragement.

Thank you to Christopher Mitchell for inviting me to his "Author Group" where he taught and encouraged a small group of us who wanted to publish books. He is an author whose books can be found at Amazon.com. His wife Stacy also recently wrote her first book. They can be reached at: www.ChangeYourLifeOvernight.com

Lily Haws spent many hours helping me tell my story and asking questions which brought out details I had not thought of adding, making the story more complete. Her hours of editing and restructuring were needed and helped the story to flow.

CHAPTER 1

MY BEGINNING

~Picking Blueberries ~

It was a beautiful morning in June, and I was picking blueberries in our backyard. My husband Ivan had gone off to his carpentry job. He tends to be a perfectionist which makes him an excellent trim carpenter. After years of carpentry experience, he is an all-round handyman – doing repairs, replacing doors and windows, and building decks.

I was enjoying the quiet time of being home alone and in deep thought as the berries dropped into my little bucket. I was filled with thankfulness for the many answered prayers we have experienced. I reflected back to nearly thirty years ago when we belonged to the Amish church with our family and friends. Leaving our Amish life was not anything we had considered. Born Amish, die Amish was the way it was done, and we had never experienced a different way.

Out of the corner of my eye, I caught a movement in the grass and turned to see a squirrel scampering across the yard only a few feet away from me. I looked around for Maggie, our dog, who would not allow trespassing critters on her territory. I approved of her keeping them out of the vegetable garden, especially the raccoon who loves our sweet corn, but Maggie was out of sight. She can roam freely over the countryside but is usually with me when I am outdoors.

I went on with my blueberry picking. Suddenly, there was a whirl and a rush in the grass. My thoughts returned to the squirrel that was in the yard. Maggie spotted it, and the chase was on to the nearest tree.

I'm sure I read more into it than was there as I saw the squirrel glance over her shoulder seeming to say with a grin, "Bet you can't catch me!" Staying just out of reach, she gave the dog the excitement of possibly winning this chase. About four feet up the tree, the squirrel paused on the opposite side, waiting till Maggie *almost* had her; she easily went on up to the safety of the tree.

I heard the words of Jesus, "I am that tree in your life. I am your safety."

The dog sat barking.

I was reminded that all of the barking and roaring threats in my life cannot reach me because I am covered by the redeeming blood of Jesus. I could imagine the squirrel resting comfortably, smiling and arms folded, if you will, in the safety of that tree.

I marveled at the thought of all the change that has taken place in thirty years.

~ Early Childhood ~

I was born in Indiana. I can still remember the dairy farm where we lived even though I was only three years old when we moved from there. We spoke what many call "Pennsylvania Dutch" or "Dutch." It is an unwritten dialect originating from the *Deitsch* (German) and passed from generation to generation.

I remember one time while playing outside, we noticed a commotion among the cows. We went over to the fence to get a better look and discovered a new calf had been born. We crawled under the fence and headed over to have a closer view, but the mother cow was unhappy with our invasion and angrily came a few steps toward us. I remember my older brother saying, "We have to talk English to these cows. They don't understand Dutch!"

My mom remembers another day at the farm. She noticed that the children had disappeared. She went to check on their safety and to see where they were. She could hear them. They were saying, "There goes another big truck!"

My three older siblings had climbed up the 80-foot silo and were watching the traffic on the highway. They hadn't let me go up with them because I was too small to reach the first rung on the ladder.

Totally frightened to see where they were, Mom halted between the urge to shout to them to get down to safety or to return to the house without a word and let them come down in their own time. If she shouted, she would possibly put fear into the little ones. She chose the latter and went back into the house on shaking legs that felt like jello. She kept a watchful eye out for them back on the ground. Sure enough, they came back into the yard, unharmed.

~ Southern Ohio ~

In the fall of 1963, we moved from Indiana to southern Ohio, where my dad intended to start a new Amish community. Most Amish were farmers back then, and though the land was less expensive, it was not good for farming. That was one reason the community never grew.

My dad was not a farmer, so the land condition did not affect him. He started a bakery. He had a hardworking wife with good management skills; the business grew to be a success. Dad was a good salesman and sold their products in nearly 70 stores.

My mother rose early in the morning and worked long days, trying to meet the endless demands. The more the business grew, the more help they hired. The more help they hired, the more she had to be there to supervise the workers.

My dad grumbled and complained, and he got worse as time went on. Mom suffered intense emotional, mental, and verbal abuse from him.

Many Amish families are good with child training and discipline. As the children work alongside their parents or older siblings, they learn valuable lessons about doing their share, taking turns, and practicing the Golden Rule. I believe that my mom's biggest regret in life is that she set the children aside for the sake of work. With the extremely high demands of the business, we children got pushed back as my mom tried hard to please my dad. She was a good, fast worker, but the more she did, the more he expected.

~ Paul's Beating ~

We were often left alone. The older children took responsibility and cared for the younger. Many times my parents were late coming in from the bakery, and many times we went to bed without them. One night we children had not gone to bed and were waiting for them to come in.

My brother Paul was probably around two or three years old and had fallen asleep on the couch. Dad did not gather this poor, sleeping child in his arms and carry him upstairs to his bed. Dad shook Paul and told him to get up and go to bed. Paul was confused and was in a stupor, not fully awake. He was frightened, trying to comprehend what he was supposed to do.

My father spanked him and said, "I told you to go to bed!" Now Paul was really frightened and crying. Dad told him to "Shut up!"

Again, Paul *disobeyed* because he did not quit crying. My father took him across his knees and soundly spanked him again. Paul continued to cry. The beating was repeated. We stood there in horror watching as an innocent little boy got a severe, unjust punishment.

Dad was determined that his child would obey. He blew in Paul's face so that Paul had to gasp for his breath. In that moment, he was *obeying*. As soon as he got his breath back, he let out another terrified scream, crying for help, only to receive another beating for *disobeying*.

This horrible scene went on and on. Finally, when Paul had no other way of releasing his emotions, he began to laugh. This was *acceptable* behavior for my father, and to our relief, the beating finally stopped.

For the next several days, Paul's bottom was black and blue. I remember Mom showing it to my dad, hoping there would be some regret or apology for his cruel actions.

"What's that?" he asked.

"It's bruises."

"What from?"

"This is from your beating the other night!" Mom said.

We could hardly believe his indifference. This kind of *child training* is one of the many types of abuse that happened in our home. Mom recalled another time when she couldn't take the baby to church because of the black and blue bruises on the baby's face.

My mom felt that she could not say or do anything because the scripture in 1 Peter 3:1 states, "…wives be in subjection to your own husbands…" The Amish take a strong stance on the woman remaining silent and obeying her husband. My father interpreted this to mean that she had NO say.

Instead of lovingly being put to bed with a prayer or a Bible story, we often went to bed dirty, not bothering to change our clothes. The next morning we got up and ran into a new day with the same clothes on.

I liked it when Mom would have food out for us. She would be working in the bakery. We ate by ourselves, again, the older taking care of the younger.

When we wanted or needed something, we would run over the broken cement slab walk to the bakery in search of Mom. Sometimes, we just wanted to be with her and watch her work, usually when Dad was not present. He felt that children *got in the way*.

We loved it when she gave us delicious bites of sweet rolls or donut holes – iced, sugared, or glazed. Sometimes we'd reach into the box of nuts or coconut and eat a handful. My father would usually chase us out. We were in the way or slowing down progress. They chased us out if a car drove in because we were often "too dirty to be seen."

When the day-olds came back from the store, we often fed them to the animals. Cows, pigs, horses, chickens, they all got the day-olds. I remember helping to open the plastic bags of the cinnamon rolls and selecting bites of icing before tossing the rest to the animals. Next might be a bit of sweet, sticky pecans or gooey coconut from the bottom of the coconut rolls. We ate all we wanted.

~ The Laundromat ~

Mom needed to use the laundromat in town while repairs were made on her wringer washer. I begged to go along with her to town. We had been out of clean clothes for too long. She said I couldn't go. I was too dirty, and she had nothing clean for me to wear.

The Amish do not have electricity or cars but will hire a neighbor to drive them into town or to other places. Our neighbor was willing to take Mom to the laundromat.

They were loading baskets and pillowcases stuffed with dirty clothes into the car. The back seat was filled. While no one was watching, I crawled into the back seat of the car and hid in the laundry. I listened to the voices of the adults. The doors banged shut, the engine started, and I was still in the car. We began to move. I was going along. I rode for a while, and then I peeked out enough to see where we were going. Soon I forgot that I was hiding and began enjoying our ride. Suddenly, the driver caught sight of me in the rearview mirror and motioned for my mother to look. It was too late to go back and make me stay at home.

As soon as she got the washers going, Mom found something for me to wear that was in better shape than what I was wearing. She marched me into the bathroom and changed my clothes. I don't remember getting punished or if I was missed at home. All that I remember is – I went along!

Later, rather than letting my mom go to the laundromat, Dad decided he would do it. Mom was needed to keep the bakery running. When he brought the laundry back, it had been taken out of the hot dryer and stuffed into baskets and boxes. Most of our homemade clothes were made of Dacron broadcloth – the wrinkles set in severely.

~ The Last Month of School ~

Three years before we moved from southern Ohio, my three oldest siblings went to a "home school" at the home of another Amish family. A month before the school year was completed, that family decided to move elsewhere. Dad chose to send the three children to an Amish community several hours away to finish the last month of school there. They were taken away to live with strangers. At the first home, the three children sat on a couch as the children from the family stood along the opposite wall, staring at them. No one said anything for a long, awkward time.

My sister had started first grade, and she was only six. It was very hard for her to be separated from our family, especially from our mother.

Because of the cruelty that my sister saw my mom suffer, she often feared that Mom would die and that we would be left alone with Dad. We were not told where babies came from. Two babies had been born at our home in southern Ohio, and we weren't told ahead of time. When the doctor showed up, we feared for Mom.

My sister remembers that she cried often while she was away. This separation broke my mom's heart too. She wrote letters to reach the hearts of her little ones. She printed the letters (not cursive) in first-grade language so that my sister could read hers by herself. Mom addressed the letters with each child's name on the envelope in care of one of the families where they stayed. When the letters were given, they had already been opened. The children felt hurt at not having the privilege of opening their own letter.

No place was homebase for the children, and they could pick where they wanted to stay each night. No one was in charge of the three; they had been left to the community. They could freely walk to one home or another, and no one stopped them.

My oldest brother adapted the best, and the younger brother and sister stayed together often. One day my sister did not want to stay where the boys stayed, so she walked to the community grandparents' house, only to find no one at home. She then walked to the house of the folks who owned a bakery – a total of five miles, alone on the gravel roads at only six years old!

One of the good times that the three remember was the field trip that they took to a museum on the last day of school. In the afternoon they were allowed to run, and they found many mushrooms on a shady bank. My sister loved to run; she liked the freedom it provided. School was over, and she was happy to be going home.

CHAPTER 2

BILLY

~ A Special Pony ~

Billy was part horse and part Shetland pony, so he was taller than a Shetland pony, yet smaller than most horses. I learned to ride on Billy, as did all of my siblings and all of my children. He lived to be 38 years old. I can remember when he was a colt and the day Dad said, "It is time to train Billy." Dad was very good at training horses, and I loved to watch.

Dad trained Billy for riding and pulling the cart. He taught him to come at the command, "Come here." It would come out as "Com'ere." Billy would do it. He knew exactly what was being asked of him. He responded beautifully. He was also smart enough to know that he *could* run away when he was in the pasture. Sometimes when we went out to catch him, he would obey when we spoke the command, "Com'ere," to him, but most times he did not. He would run away, and he was very challenging to catch.

During the morning chores, Billy came in with the rest of the horses for feeding. When we knew that we needed Billy for that day, we would keep him in the barn afterward.

When I was in my teens, we got a battery-operated electric fence. Oh, Billy hated that fence! He associated the shock of touching it with the "zitt" noise he heard and learned very quickly to respect the hot wire. When Billy was being difficult to catch, we got the great idea to corner him in the field, using a roll of electric fencing wire. Two of us would unroll the wire, pulling it taut across his path of escape. Billy thought it was a hot wire coming toward him, so he let us corner him in part of the pasture. As we got closer, we rolled up the wire to keep a tight, believable "hot" fence.

Realizing that he was about to be caught, he would sometimes try to make a dash to escape, despite our commands of "Whoa" or "Come'ere!"

So we'd make the "zitt!" sound, and he would stop in his tracks, give up, and let himself be caught.

While still living in Southern Ohio, we would hitch Billy to the cart, go out in the fields, and pick wild blackberries in the summer. We had difficulty reaching the good ones way up high, so we'd back the cart into the bushes and stand on the seat to reach the berries. I remember once when we were doing this, my oldest brother, Joe, yelled, "BEAR!"

We left that place quickly in our alarm. Joe later told us that he kept hearing a lip-smacking noise and looked to see what it was. The bear was minding his own business and enjoying his berries.

We worked and played with Billy. I liked to ride him and find a choice spot of grass. Sometimes, I would brush his coat, watch him eat, or just enjoy nature.

We rode him bareback because we didn't like the saddle, but I think Billy hated the saddle more. I wish I had a picture of five of us on his back at one time. Of course, we couldn't ride fast or far like this; we did this just for fun. Usually, a small child rode on his neck with the rest on his back. We rode him or hitched him to the buggy, the cart, the cultivator for weeding in the garden, or to the "mud boat."

The mud boat was a homemade sled with two-by-four runners and plywood for the floor, the front, and the two sides. We used the mud boat to haul things. We would also load it with manure from the barn to spread on the field for fertilizer.

We hitched Billy to the cultivator and took him through the long rows of sweet corn in the garden. Trying to stay in the middle and being careful not to run over the little plants was frustrating for both him and for us. By the time we got everything aligned, we were already at the end of the row.

Billy had the terrible habit of biting. Almost all of us had black and blue marks at some time from where he bit us. He hated the belt of the harness being tightened. We could see his anger when he would pin his ears back. Whenever his ears were pinned back, it was a good time to beware!

~ Tragedy Strikes ~

June of 1974 was a sad month; trouble came in threes for our family. My seventh brother, Mahlon, was born with complications to his internal organs, and the doctors said he would not live. He died eleven days after he was born.

The day Mahlon died, my parents hired our kind neighbor, Jeff Fletcher, to take them back to the hospital. While they were gone, my seven-year-old brother, David, was trying to catch Billy. He used an ear of corn to help coax him. David had just learned how he could get on Billy's back without needing something to stand on. He put his toes on Billy's knees, grabbed a handful of the thick mane, and pulled himself up and onto his back. David tried to get onto his back and failed while Billy was busy eating his corn. On the second attempt, Billy was extremely irritated and reached back to bite him. David reached out his hand to ward off the bite, and Billy caught the tip of David's finger and bit it completely off.

After Mahlon's death, my parents came home from the hospital. They asked the same driver to turn around and take David to the hospital. His bone was exposed, and the doctor cut it evenly. He took a patch of skin from David's wrist to graft onto his fingertip. The doctor kept repeating, "It's going to hurt one more time."

When my parents came home and had to turn around and take David to the hospital, Mom saw my brothers sliding down a long plank that they had set up from the chicken house roof to the ground. "That is too dangerous. They need to take it down," Mom told Dad.

"Aw, let em slide," he responded.

It wasn't long after that my nine-year-old brother, Daniel, tried a running start before hitting the slide. Instead, he fell off it and broke his arm which meant another trip to the hospital.

The next day David begged my mom to remove the bandage from his finger. Finally, he persuaded her when he said, "It is not the tip of my finger that hurts. It's farther down, on my hand."

Mom unwrapped it, and thankfully so. The bandage was so tight his finger was turning blue. He had immediate relief when she loosened it.

Within a two week period of time, my mom gave birth, my brother lost the tip of his finger, another broke his arm, and we had the funeral for my eleven-day-old brother.

~ Rodeo King ~

Herding cows and the horses was no problem as long as we had Billy. We would ride him, and he caught on quickly. He could stop on a dime to catch a stray. If there was a slow straggler, we'd tighten our heels into his sides and say, "Bite 'em!" And he would.

One day our English neighbor, Bud Fulmer, who did quite a bit of regular driving for my dad, pulled in with his truck and trailer to pick up a steer. "Do you have the steer in?"

"No," came the answer. "But it will be by the time you get turned around!" We had Billy in the barn and rode him down in the field. As soon as he knew which one was to be brought in, that animal had no chance to escape!

Billy was good at so many things. When we'd ride him up to a gate, he learned to stand sideways so we could reach and open the gate without getting off. Then we'd ride through, and he'd turn sideways again so we could close it again.

We could tie Billy on a long rope to eat at a spot that had no fence. Other horses would have gotten tangled in the line, but Billy was very relaxed about having a rope around his feet and usually was able to keep himself untangled.

Billy learned how to open the hook latch on one of the feed boxes. He would use his nose and help himself. After he was done, others would get into it and get sick from overeating. Billy knew his limit and never got sick.

We learned to secure the feed box, but we had to be careful with all the doors and gates. He would open them with his nose and let himself and all the others out.

Billy didn't need a bit in his mouth. We usually snapped the reins on his halter. One year our mailman suggested that Billy should be in the annual Old Fashioned Day Parade in our small town. Because we were Amish, we would not be allowed by our church to be in a parade. We told our mailman that he could drive him in the parade, and he did. The people got a kick out of the pony without a bridle.

We often went by our neighbor Mr. Norris's beautiful dairy farm. He got to know Billy pretty well, and he was amazed at Billy's obedience to stop when one called "Whoa!" One time he was in his yard close to the road as we passed by with Billy. He called out loudly, "Whoa!" Billy stopped. Mr. Norris laughed at his prank as we got Billy going again.

CHAPTER 3

THE NEW COMMUNITY

~ Not Your Grandma ~

After six years of living in southern Ohio, my family moved to a new Amish settlement. We were still in Ohio, but further north. In this small, newly-starting community, the children my age were surrounded by their parents, cousins, aunts and uncles, as well as their Grandma and Grandpa.

All of my grandparents were still living, but they lived in a different state. The five-hour trips to see them did not happen very often. I was closer to my mom's parents. We didn't see my dad's parents as often. I loved my mom's parents and found a special place in my heart for older people. I loved to hear them talk. I liked their wrinkles and their beautiful white hair.

When we first moved it seemed like the little ones around me were always saying, "Grandma…"

for this and that. Their grandma was kind and loved her family. I wanted to call her grandma too, and we referred to her as "Grandma" when my family talked about her in my home.

One Sunday afternoon I *did* call her Grandma, and one of her grandchildren heard me and lost no time in letting me know that she was NOT my Grandma.

I talked to her later when none of the other children were around to hear. I asked her if I could call her *Grandma*. To my relief and delight, the kind old lady said that I might. So I did. I didn't care anymore if her grandchildren heard me or not; I had permission.

I was nine years old when we moved. It was a strange, new experience to be with a group that talked our language and dressed as we did. One of my younger siblings pointed, "There goes a buggy!" while tugging on Mom's dress for her to look. We acted like the "Englishers."

Although we were now in an Amish community, I still felt "different." Our accent was different. They rolled their R's; we didn't. We were often told, *"Sel iss nat ve ma doot"* (That's not how it's done). Which meant: that's not how *we* Amish do things.

~ Our Play Time ~

We had much fun exploring our new home. There was an old building on the property that must have been a house at one time. We liked to dig through the layers of trash and find treasures. My sisters and I wanted to clean it out and fix it up for our playhouse. We spent many spare moments sorting and cleaning it out, burning what we could.

Our English landlord drove a big feed truck that would pull into our drive each day, bringing feed to the turkey houses which were on the back of the property. He gave a warning: "There shall not be any toys left in the drive. I WILL NOT get out and remove them."

All was well for a few weeks, and then we learned a hard lesson. Our little red wagon had been left in the drive. The landlord ran over it, crushing it beyond repair. We were devastated! We didn't have many toys.

We didn't get a new wagon until the following spring. A large box arrived. I read "Radio Flyer" on the box. I remember the "Flyer" part of the name and kept imagining how much fun we would have *flying* on that wagon.

We were not allowed to open that box "till the weather gets nice and warm." Mom said, "When the leaves begin to show green on the trees, you may open it." I had never before waited with so much impatience for the trees to be green.

My little brothers often played at the end of the lane where there was a culvert pipe. They had cleared out much of the washed in gravel, so it was large enough for them to crawl into it. One day the boys heard the big feed truck coming. One of them decided to be in the culvert while the truck ran over it. The others stood watching. Sure enough, the truck ran over the culvert with him in it, and he was fine. However, some days later two big trucks came to haul out the full-grown turkeys. After the first truck pulled in, we could hear the second one coming. Three of the little children hurried to crawl into the culvert before the second truck came. After a while, my mom wondered where these three were. She couldn't hear an answer when she called. She asked Paul if he knew where they were. "The last time I saw them was when they were running down to the culvert before the second truck came," he informed her. The second truck had driven over the end of the culvert pipe and bent it down. The three children were trapped inside and couldn't get out. The other end was plugged with dirt and gravel. A jack was needed to pry open the end to let them out. My brother Daniel said that they weren't afraid because they knew someone would come to get them out.

~ Cooler Sleeping ~

The house was not insulated. That first winter was so cold that when someone in our community butchered a cow and gave us a few pieces of beef, Mom stored some of it upstairs. It stayed frozen for days.

The house was also sweltering in the summertime. We didn't have electricity to run fans. After our parents thought we were upstairs in bed, somebody decided to go out on the flat part of the roof with a blanket.

"Is it cooler out there?"

"It sure is!"

Soon we each took a blanket and settled on the roof. Of course, our parents didn't know. One time we went over the top of the house to the other side. This roof was less steep, but the drop-off was much higher and much more dangerous. I had the constant fear of sliding down, and I couldn't relax enough to sleep, so I went back inside for the rest of the night.

The next morning Levi told us that he woke up and his feet were dangling. He didn't know where he was at first. He awoke with a start when he realized that he was ON THE EDGE OF THE ROOF! That was the first and the last time of sleeping on that part of the roof.

One time when we were retelling some of the crazy things we had done, including many things

Mom never knew, she said, "I wouldn't have any children left if the Lord hadn't been watching over them!"

~ Buggy Rides ~

We rode to church in our family buggy. This buggy had a front seat where my dad, my mom, and the youngest children would ride. The children sat on my parents' laps; they had no car seats. Behind the front seat were two bench-seats which held three on each side. These seats faced each other. The buggy had a roof and a door on the back end. Under the back door was an attached step.

We had other horses besides Billy. One was a beautiful palomino we called Pally. She would trot along until we got to a hill where she slowed to a walk. We older (and heavier) children usually jumped out and walked up the hill to lighten the load. Sometimes Mom would get off to walk too, but I don't remember Dad ever getting off.

One time when my mom was pregnant, she walked up the hill. As she was getting back on the buggy, Dad said to her, "You looked like a fat old cow walking up the hill." No one laughed.

We had an open buggy that we called the spring wagon. It was nice to use in the summertime. This buggy had no top, one seat in the front, and a bed in the back like a pickup truck. All of the older children sat in the back. The two oldest sat with their feet dangling over the back edge. The back two wheels were tall enough that part of them showed above the bed of the buggy. I remember watching the wheel right beside me, going around. The individual spokes became a blur as we went faster.

Once, while we were walking up the hills behind the spring wagon, Daniel, one of my younger brothers, selected a slender stick. At the top of the hill, he kept his stick with him as we all got back on to ride at a faster clip. Soon, he made the stick ride on top of the buggy wheel as he held it in place, liking the sound it made. Next, he rested the stick against the spokes. Now he really had a nice clickety sound going -- what fun! The sound changed according to the speed at which we traveled. Going

31

up the next hill, more of us selected slender sticks. I wasn't sure if Dad would be okay with it, but he seemed amused until we got heavier sticks that might ruin the paint job; that was the end of that.

Most of the times when we went somewhere in the buggy, Dad would grumble and complain, making it unpleasant for all of us. As soon as we arrived at our destination, he would be Mr. Pleasant, greeting everyone with a smile and pleasant words. I knew my dad was not what people outside our family thought he was and began to feel we were the only family with a dad like mine. He was an angry person and often raised his voice in anger. The angrier he got, the louder he screamed. Many times, the first thing we heard in the morning was his angry voice.

I knew that our family was different from the rest. I tried to fit in, but I noticed small things that made me think that we *were* different. I liked the color of Pally's golden coat and white mane, however, I was conscious of the fact that we were the only ones in the community with a palomino horse. So much emphasis was put on uniformity that when things were different, it was noticed. I felt small things like this helped to set us apart.

~ We Grew Our Food ~

Every summer we had a vegetable garden. The children helped with the work of planting, weeding, harvesting, and canning. We helped Mom can at least 200 quarts each of green beans, tomatoes, and peaches. We also canned around 200 quarts of vegetable soup. Other Amish families canned their meat, but we never had much meat to can.

Mom would let each of us have a small space of our own in the garden. We could plant whatever we wanted in it. Mom always had flowers in her vegetable garden, so we also wanted flowers in our small gardens too.

Some of these flowers were from seeds that she had saved from the previous year, but most reseeded themselves and came up each year with the weeds as the soil warmed up each spring. She taught us to identify plants, and we learned to transplant these little plants into rows.

We had a path to walk on, separating each small garden. We were responsible for our own little space. Some chose to be very diligent in watering the newly transplanted plants and to keep them clean of weeds, others not so much. Some of my smaller siblings were excited to have a garden and to plant it, but the burden of weeding and keeping order was not so exciting. As the weather grew hot, the love for the little garden spot grew cold.

~ Bare Necessities ~

My parents didn't go to the store very often, every month or two. When we did go, it was for things we didn't grow like sugar, flour, or salt. They also bought hardware supplies.

We didn't *think* of buying or eating a salad in the wintertime. Things were eaten in season or from what we grew in the garden and canned. Without electricity, there were no freezers.

In the first years after moving to the new community, money was tight. My parents never bought cold cereal, pop, or chips. In the winter we mainly ate oatmeal for our breakfast cereal. Sometimes Mom cooked cracked wheat or corn mush. We liked fried corn mush and put honey on it. In the summertime, we often enjoyed Mom's homemade "Grape Nuts" for a cold cereal.

After I was older, my parents began buying more groceries from the store, including boxed cereal. I remember when Mom splurged and bought some Campbell's Cream of Chicken Soup to make a casserole for company. I was learning to cook, and one day I wanted to use a can of Campbell's soup. I opened a can, and it didn't look or smell right, so I dumped it and opened another one. Spoiling would occasionally happen with our garden canned foods when the seal broke. I thought this soup was spoiled. Later, to my great regret, I found out that Mom had gotten a different kind of soup for a recipe she wanted to try, and I had dumped it! I should have read the label.

So much has changed since those days. Take strawberries for instance, we never had fresh strawberries unless they were in season. When they were beginning to ripen, we were so excited. It was an event to look forward to. Our mouths would water at the thought of fresh berries and all the ways we would eat them. We made pies. We ate them mashed and sweetened, poured over shortcake, chocolate cake, cookies or, of course, homemade ice cream. Whatever we didn't eat fresh, Mom made into jam. She always made a variety of jams and apple butter.

Now strawberries can be bought all year long. When they are beginning to ripen here in Ohio it's really no big deal. We even hear our children groan at the thought of picking them.

~ Carrying Water ~

We had no plumbing in the house for the first several years, so we carried many gallons of water from the spring. We had little gallon buckets, and it seemed like an endless job to fill the big iron kettle that sat in the yard.

Mom would build a fire under the kettle to heat the water for Monday's laundry and again on Saturdays for baths. To this day when I smell the smoke of a wood fire, especially on a summer evening, it reminds me of the bathwater heating.

We learned to spare water. It is hard for me to have water running in the sink. Some folks let it run while washing dishes and while rinsing them. All those gallons of good, clean water down the drain! It feels like such a waste to me.

When we first moved to the Amish community, the water from the spring flowed in a marshy creek across the yard to the lane. Dad made a cement tank in the ground beside the lane, deep enough to set the ten-gallon milk cans into for cooling. The tank could fit two milk cans side by side, and it was eight or ten feet long. The spring water was tiled with a four-inch pipe that flowed into the tank. The overflow ran out the other end. We kept our milk cooled this way. Later, a milk house was built over that tank. There was a huge bank between the house and the road, and this was leveled. The dirt covered over the pipe and made a nice yard.

We also used the water for refrigerating food. Cold, spring water flowed from that four-inch pipe. Mom put leftovers in sealed containers and sent us on many, many trips to the spring to take or fetch food for her.

Once we had the cement tank, we often hitched Billy to the cart for hauling water from it. I had Billy hitched to the cart one day before the milk house was built, and I backed him right up to the platform beside the cement water tank. While I was filling the cans, Billy decided to walk forward a few steps across the lane to eat the grass on the other side, taking the cart with him. I let him munch until I had the cans filled then I said, "Back up, Billy." Billy hated to back up.

I repeated, "Back up!"

He pinned his ears back, and he backed up -- FAST! I was standing between the tank and the cans. Before I knew it, the cart bumped into the cans, dumping them, and me, into the tank. Billy took off running to the barn, still hitched to the cart. It felt like he was laughing at his prank all the way.

Chapter 4

SCHOOL

~ First Grade ~

I started first grade when we still lived in southern Ohio. We hitched Billy to the cart, and the four of us went five miles to the teacher's house for school. The teacher lived with her parents, one sister, two brothers, and a friendly old grandpa whom they called "Pops." Every morning we had a Bible story and sang songs. The whole family sang in beautiful harmony. We all enjoyed the singing, and Pops would want to sing more than our usual three.

I liked everything about school except Sport, the family's beagle. That dog knew I was afraid of him. He would bear his teeth on one side and growl at me. My teacher said, "He only does that because you are afraid of him." She made me pet him and tried to make us be friends. One day in the spring, I decided to run to the outhouse, but Sport was right in my path. I startled him as much as he did me. It was too far to run back, so I quickly decided on the spot, *I won't be afraid.*

I squatted down and held my hand to him, "Come on, Sport!"

He came, and we were friends. He never growled at me again.

One morning we came to a "Road Closed" sign. There was no way we were going to get to school if we had to take another way. I thought there was nothing to do but turn around and go home. My oldest brother Joe was wiser than I, "Let's at least go see where it's closed and why it's closed. We can always turn around and go home from there if we have to. At least we will know why it is closed and maybe find out for how long."

As we approached the place where the men were working, we saw that they were replacing a culvert. Again, I didn't know what we could do. The men were very kind to us. They asked if we knew how to "unhook" our horse, and Joe said that we did. The men took some planks, put them over the creek where the road was missing, and helped us pull the cart across.

"Here, Honey, take my hand," one of the workers said, as he assisted my walk over the plank. When it was my sister's turn, she refused help and demonstrated her ability to cross unassisted.

Joe hopped on Billy's back and rode him through the creek. On the other side, we hitched Billy up again. The men told us that they would be done before we had to head home. Sure enough, the new culvert was in that evening.

Billy could be a real slowpoke. We had a whip to keep his pace up. He would spy a nice clump of clover and stop for a bite if the driver didn't keep him on track. In the winter time, Joe always held the reins, so my brother Levi would hold the whip. He liked to use it a little too much. Joe had to tell him, "The only time you are allowed to use it is when I say '*fitz*'" (whip). It didn't take long for Billy to learn what *fitz* meant. The actual whip wasn't needed anymore!

Another thing Billy learned on those school trips was the sound of the Slow Moving Vehicle emblem falling off. It happened often, and each time it did, Joe called out, "Whoa!" Billy was always happy to stop. After a few times of this happening, Billy caught on and would stop automatically.

There was a time that Billy needed shoes, and Dad didn't get them on him. That morning, we had to walk the five miles to school. Soon after we started for home that night, a black car passed us and then turned around and slowly passed us again. We were prepared to say "No, thank you," to a stranger offering us a ride. The car came back a third time, and the man driving pointed at my oldest sister. She was eight years old. We had a creepy feeling as he drove on again. That scared us!

A little later, we heard the sound of a vehicle approaching; fear struck all of us instantly. Joe said, "RUN!" and we all ran into the cornfield. I couldn't see it, but Joe said it was the same car. We walked through the cornfield back to the school. We never wanted to see that car again. Our teacher's brother drove us home that night.

~ School in the New Community ~

We moved in 1969, and I started the third grade that fall. That same year the first schoolhouse for our community was built. They named it West View because it was on top of a steep hill with a good view to the west. Most Amish children walk to school, and after we moved we started walking to school. We lived farther away from the school than most of the other kids, but for the first two years we walked the three miles to school. After we walked those three miles to school, we still had to climb that steep hill each morning. Later, Dad took the job of teaching, and we used the horse and buggy for transportation.

When the parents met to discuss what curriculum would be used, my parents suggested "Rod and Staff." We had used it before moving. It is a Bible-based curriculum. The first word that first graders learn is "GOD." It was voted down. One of the parents even said, "We can't have that. Soon our children would know more about the Bible than we do!" They chose an Amish curriculum instead.

Just as Satan influenced men to take God out of the public schools, so he is weaving his dark thread through the Amish. If he can cause them to pay more attention to *their* rules than God's – who is winning here? At one time in this same church community, some of the leaders that held more strictly to the ways of the forefathers ruled that a female teacher was not allowed to teach or explain the Bible in their school. A man could, but not a female. She was not even allowed to lead the Lord's Prayer in front of her students.

~ Traditional Amish School ~

An Amish education starts when a child is six or seven, and it ends in the eighth grade. Students are usually in a one-room schoolhouse, and all the grades are taught by a teacher with an eighth-grade education.

Because families speak the Pennsylvania Dutch dialect at home, we learned English at school. We picked up some English words before then, but primarily, Amish children learn to speak English at the start of their schooling along with reading, writing, arithmetic, and some history. Education and child training are viewed as the responsibility of the parents; Amish do not have preschools.

Our chores had to be done before we went to school. The younger children slept in a bit longer. After chores were done, we headed to the house where Mom had a hot breakfast ready. The younger children were up and dressed by then. We all sat down to eat together before heading off to school, lunch bucket in hand.

Sometimes at school, some of the other children brought sandwiches made with canned hamburger for lunch. They looked so good. To make a warm sandwich on cold winter days, they wrapped a slice in foil and placed it on the pipe coming from the furnace in the basement. The smell of it made my mouth water for a bite.

I asked Mom to fix two slices of bread with ketchup on them because I wanted to pretend that I had meat too. The first day of the ketchup sandwich, I thought it was good. The next day the bread was dry, and my imagination was too.

We had no use for shoes in the summertime. The skin on our feet grew tough, and we could run on gravel without it hurting. We went to church and school barefooted.

At recess, when the weather was warm, the boys always wanted to play softball. We did play other games like Red Rover, Freeze Tag, and Dare Base. On cold winter days, we girls usually played board games upstairs, and the boys had a rough game of Dodgeball in the basement.

Sixth grade was a turning point in my life, and it eased me out of some of my feelings of inferiority. My teacher that year made me feel like an equal. He liked my spelling, writing, and art. I didn't feel like he had a prejudiced view of my worthlessness. Because of my low self-esteem, I had not enjoyed school up until that point. He made the last three years of school a better experience for me.

One night when I was in the eighth grade, we were walking home from school and had another scare. I was the oldest and had been walking ahead of the rest of our group. As we approached the one lane bridge on Frasher Road, I saw a car parked on that bridge. A man was out of his car looking down into the water. There was no way to get around him. I started to go back, keeping my eyes on him.

Children from two other families were walking with us. Before I could warn all of them, the man heard the chatter and looked up instantly, as if he was expecting us. That scared me, and I ran back and told them to be quiet. The group split. One family went home through the woods on the left. We took off into the field to the right. We were a good distance into the field when that car drove up the road slowly toward the place where we had been minutes earlier. Afraid to walk on the road, we trudged home through the fields that night.

CHAPTER 5

CHURCH

~ Ordnung ~

There are many varieties of Amish, each differing in the *Ordnung* practiced. *Ordnung* is the German word for "order". It is the written rules that each church member agrees to live by. Each church district is lead by the bishop. He is responsible for administering discipline, marrying couples, and baptizing new members. The bishop is also responsible, to a degree, for regulating any changes to the *Ordnung* for his district. Because each district has different practices, I will write about the ones used in the community where I grew up.

The Amish do not have a separate building set aside for church. Instead, they meet in homes. Some of the largest houses or large, heated buildings are the chosen place for the gathering during the wintertime. The members whose houses are small, take their turn in the summertime, usually providing a large outbuilding, such as a shed or a barn.

When I was a young teenager, my community grew large enough that they agreed to divide the church into two districts. The main road through the community was the dividing line, making the East district and the West district. Each district held its church service every other Sunday on alternating Sundays. When the East district had church, the West district did not.

Neighbors helped each other to clean the place thoroughly where church was to be held. The men prepared the barn and outbuildings, and the women cleaned the house from top to bottom. Some of the neighbor ladies and older girls would come to help on several days, washing walls, floors, and windows. In the summer, the yard and garden were weeded and trimmed to be in tip-top condition. Everyone took turns and helped the hosting family prepare when church was at their house.

A church wagon, pulled by two heavy workhorses, carried supplies needed, such as the benches, songbooks, and dishes. The handmade benches that were stored on this wagon had folding legs. They came in several lengths, four-feet, six-feet, and ten-feet long, to be able to fit the different locations. The wagon stayed at the home where the church services were last held. When that family's turn was finished, the wagon went to the next place.

Preparation was made for the horses and buggy parking. The buggies were parked in rows, so as not to block access of anyone leaving. I have seen two hay wagons parked in the barn lot with horses tied side by side all around it. An outsider would wonder how the right horse gets to the right owner and buggy. They do it all the time; it is not a problem at all.

During the church service, the men sat on one side and the women on the other, facing each other on wooden benches. The girls sat in front of the women near the center of the group. The boys sat behind the men along the outer wall. The preacher stood near the center, and the congregation turned to face him.

~ The Service ~

The service began at nine in the morning and went until noon. The Bible reading was in German. The preaching was in the Amish dialect with German and English words sprinkled in, as the language is being lost to some degree. The preacher did not have a pulpit or a Bible and notes. His message was simply preached from the memory of his preparation.

Everything in each Sunday service was done very traditionally, in the same predictable way. People filed in, usually by age. Songbooks were passed out, two people sharing one book. The service started with a song. It was sung very slowly and could take ten to fifteen minutes.

Three men conducted the service. The first of the preachers stood to his feet and began with a greeting. He would then enter into his sermon. When he was done, another person, usually a deacon, would read the selected chapter from the Bible. The second preacher followed the reading with the main sermon. Familiar verses are quoted by all the preachers every Sunday.

Preachers were chosen by lot. Some were gifted and animated and would walk around when they spoke. Others, not so much, and they struggled. Often the youth found a church service hard to endure with the regular repetition of the three-hour tradition. It grew monotonous, and they were bored.

One of my brothers told me how the boys would occasionally break the boredom during church. They would catch a fly, tie the longest hair that they could find on it, and then they let it go. They would get the hair ready with a loop that only needed tightening. After a fly was caught, they put its body through the loop and tightened it, keeping hold of the other end. They let it fly like a kite. At other times, they would select a piece of hay or straw from the barn floor and braid it, or they would use it to tickle the guy who had fallen asleep. He would rub at it thinking it was a fly. None of this was acceptable behavior. They knew they had to act very quietly with no laughing, and it was a sure sign to quit if actions caused heads to turn.

After the preaching ended, several preachers and sometimes older men were asked to witness that what was preached was true to the Bible. The announcements were then made, such as where they planned to meet in two weeks or perhaps an upcoming wedding, etc. Sometimes church business was done, and the unbaptized youth were excused while the members remained for the meeting.

After the service the men helped each other quickly convert the benches into tables with "leg-extenders," two benches side by side making a table. A meal was served after the church service. We usually had bean or potato soup, especially in the winter. I remember having pickles or pickled beets, homemade bread – sometimes with sliced meat and cheese or peanut butter or sometimes apple butter.

The children played after the meal while the adults visited. Many of the women and older girls cleared away the food and washed the dishes. For the most part, the men and women stayed in their own groups to eat and visit.

On Sunday evenings, we always had a hymn singing for the youth group. The family hosting the church service served the evening meal to them. After the meal, the youth sang for an hour. Our song books were German, and we used tunes from English songs we knew such as *What a Friend we Have in Jesus.* We fit the tunes onto the German words because we were not allowed to sing in English. We *were* allowed to sing faster than we did in the church service where we sang our hymns very slowly.

~ Outsiders ~

Many people want to know if outsiders ever become Amish. They do, but rarely. The language is a challenging barrier. Also, the tight-woven Amish traditions which are passed from generation to generation create a disadvantage for the outsider.

My paternal grandparents took in a girl, named Pearl, who came from an abusive home. They started to feed her, and eventually, Pearl came to live with them, went to church with them, learned the language, and wore the clothes. But every time she gave her name at introductions, people asked "Pearl?" They wanted more information because they knew that wasn't an Amish name. So she changed her name to Katie, and she was able to blend in better.

Most Amish can make some connection through a line of relatives and quickly recognize a new name. There are also the culture, traditions, and rules to learn. An outsider has trouble blending in.

~ In-Between Sundays ~

With our district having church services every other Sunday, we were free to visit in the other districts on the in-between Sunday. Sometimes, a family invited one or more families to share a meal together. Some just quietly spent the day relaxing.

At our house, the in-between Sundays were not pleasant. After the breakfast dishes and the other morning housework was completed, our tradition of

Rishta fa da dawg (prepare for the day) was to read the Bible. In my early childhood, we didn't have a church because there were not enough families in the community. Before they moved to another community, one other Amish family lived nearby so we got together on Sundays and had a Bible story and sang a few songs. After we moved to the new community, Dad still started the in-between Sunday with Bible reading and singing. He made us pick a song then lead in singing it, but he was easily irritated. We never knew what might set him off. As much as I liked singing, I hated to be forced to sing in this atmosphere. Eventually, we quit singing the songs on Sundays.

When I was young, we would also write a letter to my *Dawdys* (grandparents) on my dad's side, on these Sundays. Dad gave the assignment of the letter writing but did not assist much with our continual questions of "How do ya spell…?" Mom helped us while he caught up with some reading or went for a nap.

Sometimes on nice summer days, we could get up and get the chores done before Dad got up. We would tip-toe into the kitchen and quickly grab some food, slipping out quietly. We often headed to the woods. We went far enough so that we could not hear our names if we were called. The whole day was spent out and away. Many times we would get on our horses and go riding. I loved riding without a saddle, with the wind in my face and flying at top speed.

Another acceptable excuse to get out of the house on these in-between Sundays was to go to a church service. When I got older, my brother Levi and I would sometimes go to church in another district.

~ Enos Byler ~

One of the boys in our neighborhood, Enos Byler, was more fun than most. The adults did not always appreciate his *fun*. He often got into trouble. Sometimes on our in-between Sundays, we would arrange to have company over. As long as we had company at the house, Dad would be civil, and life was more agreeable and fun.

On one summer Sunday, the Bylers and another family shared the Sunday noon meal with us. After the meal the children played outside while the parents visited.

David, one of my younger brothers, came running to where we girls were, "Enos is getting ready to jump out of the barn window!"

The other little boys were excited, standing where they would be in full sight of this stunt, eagerly waiting for the action.

"How can that be possible?" I wondered in amazement. "You mean the top window by the roof?"

I remembered how I had jumped off a low roof, probably an eight or ten-foot drop. I had lingered at the edge of that roof, very afraid of the jump, yet wanting very much to do it. Finally, I jumped. The ground seemed to slam into me as the air thumped out of me.

Now Enos was going to jump out of the top barn window! *Well, he would be the one to do it,* I concluded to myself.

"Yep, he is going to do it!" David declared as he ran back to the little group of onlookers. "If you want to see the jump, ya better be watching, or you'll miss it!" He called over his shoulder excitedly as he headed back to the group of boys.

Some of the girls ran to tell the moms who came to the door to watch. They were too late to put a stop to it, as one of his boots appeared at the loft window, way up high. After a few breathless seconds, the second boot appeared – just as his white-faced mom appeared in the doorway. A split second later, WHOOSH! Out he flew, and down, down he went! THUD!

His mom nearly fainted, knowing this was too much. He had really gotten himself hurt badly this time -- if he made it through this one alive.

Well, he did make it out alive -- even uninjured. How? What the boys had *really* done was to stuff Enos's clothes with hay and tie his boots onto his pants to be more convincing. What a relief that it was only a stuffed dummy!

Chapter 6

LIFE AT MY HOME

~ The Amish Prayer Book ~

Like most Amish families, we used the German Prayer Book. Many Amish fathers memorized the most often used prayers and could recite them without using the book. Most of these prayers included the Lord's Prayer within them, usually at the end. We'd use the prayer book every morning and again in the evening before going to bed. At night we read a chapter of the Bible followed by a prayer. We called it *Rishta fa s' bet* (preparation for bed).

In my early childhood, because we didn't understand what my dad was saying in German when we knelt for prayer, we children called it "Hee-mon Haw-men." That was our made-up phrase for what it sounded like to us. When we were called together for *Rishta* the older children called to the younger ones, "Hey, boys, come in here." As they looked up to question "Why?" The explanation came, "Hee-mon Haw-men," and it was perfectly understood what was expected.

I liked to hear Mom read the Bible for our *Rishta*, especially the stories of Jesus. I would imagine that I was there. We felt safe to ask her questions, but we learned to ask her when Dad didn't hear. He would try to outdo her or criticize what she said or how she said it.

Mom taught us about God and how to pray from the heart. She said if we are to talk to God as our Father, surely we should talk to him from our heart. I remember one day she said, "How would I feel if you came to me, reading your request out of a book? Surely God feels the same way. And if you came daily, saying the same thing each day, how would that feel?"

"Yes, but I'm not sure how to say what I want or need to say," I replied.

"God knows that too. Talk to Him just like you talk to me. God knows everything. He knows the number of hairs on your head. Give it time and practice." She taught us that God is love and has a great love for us, His children.

~ Mealtimes ~

We had three meals a day. Everyone was expected to be at the table at a set time. Each morning everyone knelt for an audible prayer from the prayer book. At the noon meal, called dinner, and at the evening meal, called supper, everyone closed their eyes for a silent prayer before and after the meal. It was a daily ritual, and everyone knew what was expected, right down to the wee ones. When I was little, the silent prayer was a signal that we could begin eating, and it signaled when we were allowed to leave after eating. It is amazing how quiet a large group could get for the silent prayer. Even the very little ones were used to this and knew to be quiet.

In many homes, this setting can be the perfect time for strong family ties to be made, a time for talking and laughing. Mom was a great cook, and we enjoyed her wonderful meals. But mealtimes at our house were not pleasant. We learned not to talk at the table. If we did say something, Dad found fault, either with the content of what was said, or how we said it. Sometimes he found fault if we used an English word where he thought it should be Dutch. Many meals were eaten in silence.

We developed our own silent sign language to communicate with each other at the table. If a throat was cleared, it was a sign to look up. One would point or make a motion sign to pass the bread, milk, or whatever one needed. There were times Dad expressed irritation that we didn't talk.

At one meal Dad was preoccupied. Someone said something, and Dad didn't respond, so another dared to speak. Soon we felt safe and began to loosen and even chattered as we would have if Dad hadn't been home. Suddenly, Dad tuned in. I remember him asking a question, and he didn't like the answer. He was furious and got up saying how we were all such a hopeless bunch of trash. With his hand, he hit each child on the head. If the head was ducked to avoid the blow, he hit our shoulder. He went around the table. When he came to Mom he lifted his hand as if to hit her as well. He hesitated as if struggling whether or not to strike. I held my breath. Surely, he dared not hit her! He didn't. Neither did he hit the youngest child who was seated in a high chair between him and Mom.

~ The Diaper ~

One warm, summer day, Mom went to town leaving my sister and me to prepare the noon meal and to serve it. After the dishes were washed, we could spend our time however we wanted until she returned.

We knew what we wanted to do. We children had been working in the creek that summer, moving rocks and dirt to dam it up a bit so we'd have a "pond" to play in. We had to take care of the younger children, so we got everybody ready to head to the creek for some splashing fun and cooling off. Just before leaving, the toddler had a soiled diaper which we quickly changed before setting off. In our haste to be gone, we left the soiled diaper folded in a heap on the porch.

We were well into our fun when we heard Dad's angry voice, "Hey!" He shouted, "Get up here right NOW!" Everybody got out of the water, and we went to see what we had done wrong.

"What do you want?"

"*Grik de fa shi-sa vin-dol* (get that soiled diaper) ...off the porch!"

That was it? We had to stop our fun immediately for *a soiled diaper*? Going to the porch, we saw that he had unrolled the diaper and left it to lay open in full sight, making it look bad indeed.

It seems he had a hard time letting us enjoy ourselves. What made him enjoy our pain? Did he feel more "in charge" when we cried or showed emotion? Is that what it took for him to feel like he was effective or in control?

~ Milking ~

We had one milk cow named Joy for our family's needs. In 1973, Dad bought eight cows, and we began to sell milk. When we first got the cows, he was involved in the barn at chore time. It was not long until we took over the responsibility, and he occupied himself with other things.

In the winter it was dark when we headed to the barn, swinging a gas Coleman lantern, feeding the animals, and milking the cows by hand. The lantern was poor light compared to electric lights.

The cats would sit nearby as we milked the cows. Each time someone got to their feet after finishing a cow, the cats meowed, begging for some warm milk in their bowl. We had a cat that stood near a cow being milked, impatiently meowing for milk. Finally, a squirt of milk was aimed at the cat. She quickly began to lick the milk from her coat. But after this was repeated over a few times we could tell she actually liked being squirted, and she tried to catch the squirt with her tongue. Amused, we started to aim a straight, steady stream to her and enjoyed watching her catch it. After some time we aimed the stream higher above her head, and to the delight of everyone watching, the cat stood on her two hind feet to catch it.

~ Our Clothes ~

Most of our clothes were homemade, but we bought socks and underwear. We women wore solid-colored, one-piece dresses with long sleeves and a loose-fitting cape. The cape is an extra part of a woman's attire intended for modesty. It is non form-fitting and worn over the top of the dress from shoulder to waist, covering the front and back A woman's cape is fastened with straight pins to an apron that is worn in the front of the dress. Our clothes had no buttons, snaps, hooks, or zippers. Women usually used straight pins for fastenings; children and men were allowed to have buttons. I used safety pins in my work dress and in unseen places on my Sunday dress.

We only had one style of dress. New dresses were worn for going to church, etc. When they became faded or worn, we used them for everyday work clothes until they wore out. The only variety I had for any of my dresses was in color or type of fabric, and both of these were limited according to our *Ordnung*. I could wear blue, all shades from dark to royal, but I could not have light blue. The same was true with green - dark was okay, but light was not. I also had brown, grey, and black. I never saw red, yellow, orange, white, purple, or lavender in my community, and they had to be made out of Dacron or other approved materials.

Men could have lighter color shirts, plus white. They had two buttons on the shirt front. Having buttons all the way down was not allowed. They had to wear suspenders -- they had to form a Y across the back, instead of crossing like an X.

Our apron belt had to be one inch wide. The dress was one piece (skirt attached - not separate). The skirt had to be in pleats (not gathered), and the pleats had to be one inch wide. The length was seven inches from the floor on a grown woman.

There were so many precise rules about clothing. I have been away long enough that I don't remember all the details. I do remember that bags of clothes were sometimes given to us by some English. Going through them was fun. Once, I found a purple sweater -- just my size. I put it on and was amazed at the comfort. Nothing was bulky or binding like some of my clothes, especially when wearing layers for warmth. I didn't want to take that sweater off, and I wore it around the house for several days. Dad, if he even noticed, didn't say a word against it, but Mom warned me not to be seen by anyone (other Amish outside our family) wearing it. Finally, it was dirty, and I took it off and put it in the dirty laundry. That was the last time I saw it.

I wondered why, if we wanted to live a simple life, we couldn't *simply* wear free clothes that were given to us. But our outward appearance had to be maintained. Some of these clothes were ripped to rags for cleaning. Mom was a good seamstress and could convert some of them to fit the standard of our *Ordnung*. Men's shirts were the main thing she could use from these English clothes. Only the buttons could be saved on some of them.

Chapter 7

THE SECOND BAKERY

My parents had a huge success with the bakery while we lived in southern Ohio. They sold bread, dinner rolls, sweet rolls, and donuts. I don't remember any cakes, pies, or cookies. My mom worked many long hours in that bakery. She was an early riser; Dad was not. He often roused Mom from sleep, urging her "to get the bread dough started" while he caught another nap.

Her hands developed sores around her fingernails. The doctor said it was a fungus from the yeast and from the moisture of all the dough she handled, but she dared not stop. She wore rubber gloves for some of the dough handling, but that made things slower and was clumsy. The products were in high demand, and Dad urged her on.

When we moved to the northern Amish community, my parents agreed to discontinue the bakery business, as there was a family in the community already operating a bakery. Dad felt that there was nothing to do but try his hand at carpentry. It was not a good fit for him, and money was very tight.

People came to the house to talk about jobs for my dad's carpentry business and asked what the wonderful smell was that filled the house. Mom made "Grape Nuts" for our breakfast cereal, and time and again she would ask, "Would you like a sample?" They would take a sample and come back later to ask if they could buy some.

In toasting the cereal, many times some of it got toasted too dark, and it couldn't be sold. She had been making white bread for the family. She decided to add some of the too dark cereal into the bread dough. It ended up making the most delicious bread we ever had.

Soon more and more people came for cereal, and Mom struggled to meet the demand from her kitchen. Dad said, "If cereal is what the people want, let's make cereal." Arrangements were made with the folks in the community who owned the bakery. My parents started to use the bakery one day a week. The demand grew, and Dad wanted to build his own bakery, but Mom said, "No." She did not want to slave away in another bakery. She was pregnant with her ninth child, and she couldn't stand the thought of leaving another baby crying in the house because of a demanding bakery. Mom was still not willing to be so tied down, and said, "If you want a bakery again, it's on you, leave me out of it."

From what I remember, the bakery was built in 1970. It was at a time when natural or organic, ready-to-eat cereals were first becoming popular. Dad put much effort into this business. They used no electricity, so he bought a diesel engine to run the equipment – a fan, the mixer, and even a hammer mill to grind the organic wheat fresh before using. He hired a mechanical engineer to make a toaster.

The first week in the new bakery Mom was looking at the new toaster invention and noticed that there was a lot of heat directed at the ceiling. "Isn't that dangerous with all that heat on the ceiling?" she asked.

"Oh, no," Dad said, "It couldn't burn."

That very night Mom woke up hearing a cracking sound. She got up to check and saw the bakery filled with flames. I had never seen a fire so hot. I watched as the glass of the windows turned to liquid, melting in the fierce heat. There was a strong wind that blew the heat away from the house. By the time the fire department came, it was too late.

I remembered a poem Mom had read to us, "Mothers only Cry at Night." I knew a lot of her sadness, and I knew she cried. That night of the fire was the first time I saw my mom cry.

~ Rebuilding ~

In 1971 the bakery was rebuilt. Our family's cereal business started again and grew over the years. To make "Grape Nuts," we first make a wheat cake. The cake was then ground into crumbs, and the crumbs were toasted. The crumbs fell from the grinder onto a conveyor belt which was about a foot wide by 25 feet long. Above the belt was a row of burners, toasting it from the top. At the end of the belt, the cereal then fell into a large stainless steel cylinder that turned around and around. It was about three feet in diameter and twenty to twenty-five feet long with burners under it. Inside this barrel were blades at an angle which tossed the cereal to the other end. The cereal fell from the tumbling stainless steel toaster into an auger. The auger took it to a belt with "cups" that took it upstairs and dumped it into a large bin. The bin could be opened on the bottom, to gravity flow from this opening into a big bowl on wheels. Then we pushed the bowl to a table and scales. There we scooped the cereal into labeled bags and tied each bag with a twist tie and put the bags into boxes.

Before the fire, the cereal business was making money. By the time a new building was up and running, General Mills had sent a notice saying that we could not call the cereal Grape Nuts because it was their patented name. We changed the name to "Wonder Crunch." When our cereal hit the market again, the cost of making it had gone up, and it had the competition of seven other new natural and organic cereals. With a new name, people did not recognize our cereal anymore.

After a few years of making Wonder Crunch, we also started to make a granola cereal, which we called "Country Lane." Then we created a third kind by mixing the two and called this mixed cereal "Country Crunch."

I worked in the bakery after school, weighing and packaging cereal, wrapping bread, labeling bags and boxes, and washing pans. There was a never-ending amount of cleaning. In 1974 I finished the eighth grade of school. I joined an older brother and sister and took my share of the responsibility of the daily work in the bakery, week after week. We made tons of cereal and hundreds of loaves of bread. I worked another seven years until I was married in 1981.

Gradually, the momentum built up again, and the orders came in. Dad hired Amish girls to help with the work. The cereal was packed in one pound bags and sold for $.69 and in five-pound bags for $3.15. Then we packed fifteen pounds into cardboard boxes. Many cases were shipped out by UPS, and many stores sold it.

Dad hired a man named Henry to deliver our cereal to the stores. Many times when the delivery man came we formed a human chain and tossed the cases to each other all the way out the door to Henry, who loaded them into his truck.

One day Levi decided to play a trick on Henry and taped an empty box shut and sent it down the line. We all were aware of the empty box except Henry. We handled it as though it was the same weight as the full ones. When Henry caught the box, it went up in the air! He caught it again, and we all laughed as he threw the empty box back into the bakery.

~ Pretty Dishes ~

Most of the Amish homes in our community had a china hutch with glass doors on the top part displaying pretty dishes. Our long tables were attractive when company came, and the prettiest dishes were used. A young girl would collect them and store them in a hope chest along with useful items that she hoped to use in her own home one day.

Near Christmas time in 1973, Dad bought some beautiful new china. He brought it in a cardboard box to show to the two girls who worked in our family bakery. To his satisfaction, we all thought it very pretty! There was an assortment of colorful flower prints on a white background. He asked the girls to choose the one they liked best.

The girls were slightly older than I was, and I worked with them daily. There were more dishes than girls, and I actually thought that I was included. Suddenly, I realized that Dad was giving these to the hired help, and I was not included. He let me know I was to *get back!* I don't remember the exact words used, but I understood that I needed *to get out of his way.*

When I realized this was only for the hired girls, it hurt. I needed to get away. I was humiliated, and my heart was broken again. I wanted to go somewhere away to disappear.

I left the bakery, tears blurring my vision. I was bursting with anger and did not want to see anyone or to be seen by anyone. Where could I run? Down was easier and faster, so I took the direction of our basement. The banks around our three-story house, dropped down on the front side, allowing a ground level entrance to the basement.

I opened the door and slipped inside as the tears burst out. Mom's wringer washer stood to my left in that front room which had large windows letting in a generous amount of light. The windows faced the north toward the gravel road that ran past our house.

I sought darkness, so I went into the next room where Mom's shelves for canned goods were built along the three walls. Tiny windows at the top of the walls on the south side let in a small amount of light.

Glancing at the stairs that led up to the kitchen, I thought that someone might come and threaten the privacy I wanted. Then I thought of the backroom! It was damp and dirty with cobwebs. Potatoes and bulbs were stored in this room. It felt like the best place to cry. I crumpled on the cold, dirty floor and let the tears flow. "Why?" I was crushed and angry at being rejected by my father once again.

In the root cellar, I was nearly cried out but still angry. I wished there were a deep, dark hole I could crawl into and never come out again! It was a sunny day, and the dark room had a small window letting in a sunbeam of light for a short period each day. I felt almost angry that the sunlight would *dare* shine in so brightly when my world was so dark, sad, and hopeless.

As I looked out the tiny window, I could see a tree outside and the bright blue sky with fluffy, white clouds. Somehow, I could feel God, and I remembered my mom telling us that God loves us and that God sees everything. Nothing is hidden from His all-knowing eyes. The beauty of nature declared the sureness of a sovereign creator. As my thoughts turned to God, I felt His presence and His love. It seemed to flow in on that bright sunlight.

~ A Trip to the Zoo ~

One summer, Dad decided to take the girls who worked in our bakery to the zoo. As the plans were made for this trip, the girls found out that Mom was not included. One of the girls told him that they would not go if my mom did not go, so he included her. She took two or three of my youngest siblings along too.

All through the day, Mom took care of her little ones. The girls could walk faster than Mom and her children; some even ran to places. Dad stayed with the girls all day, laughing and talking to them. He even ran with them, leaving Mom to care for the little ones by herself. All day long, he let her feel how much of an inconvenience she was to be included on this trip. Even today, the thought of going to the zoo is distasteful to her.

~ The Bakery is Sold ~

The summer of 1981, we shut the bakery down when my sister and I got married. By this time we older children had taken the responsibility of running the bakery. Dad bought the supplies and gave us the weekly orders. After our weddings, Dad's free labor was gone, and my younger brothers who were still living at home didn't want to work there. Dad hired more young Amish girls to help, but they didn't know how to run the business like we had. So Dad sold the business. I was glad to leave home, but I found myself grieving for *what could have been* as I saw our family business decline.

Chapter 8

FORGIVENESS

~ Trust Broken ~

From a young age, I felt a deep need to have a dad. I was most pleased with my dad when he was nice to others outside of our family. He was pleasant and seemed to be well-liked. I had a very strong desire to be liked, wanted, and accepted by him. I wanted to know that I was loved. I wanted his affirmation, but when I was eleven years old, I suffered wrong attention from my father.

Dad had hired someone to level the front yard between the house and the road. There was a big oak tree that had to be removed because it was in the way. After a great deal of effort, he had started a fire in the big stump. The whole family had worked hard that day cleaning up the brush and twigs and then adding it to the fire to burn.

That evening we had gathered in the living room, waiting for Dad to do the usual evening prayer. We were not permitted to go to bed until after he read the prayer from the German Prayer Book. It was dark outside, and before the prayer Dad said, "I wonder if we can still see any trace of the fire in the stump." He got up to go into the dark dining room to look out the window. Several of the younger siblings and I raced to the window. There was still an orange glow.

Dad came up behind me. "Sure enough," he said as he reached both hands around on my breasts, picked me up, and swung me around to let me loose as everyone headed back to the other room.

I knelt with the rest of the family, as Dad *Hee-mon Haw-men-ed* through the family ritual. I was shaken and numb with disbelief. Prayer was the farthest thing from my mind as anger and shock surged through me.

As soon as the prayer was over, my siblings began the normal race up the stairs. Burning with deep shame and anger, I headed upstairs too. I knew

I could never trust my dad again, and I was very hurt and sad.

I shared a bed with my sister who is a year older than I. She and I were always together working, singing, and playing. We usually talked and shared our hearts with each other. That night, because of the awful shame and hurt, I said nothing to her. I lay in the dark, tense with anger, wondering what I had done to deserve such treatment. Sleep would not come to me for a long time. As the sound of even breathing came from my sister, silent tears trickled down my cheeks in the dark.

One evening several weeks later, my sister and I had gone upstairs and lit our kerosene lamp. We got books, jumped into bed, and started reading a bit before sleeping. I had a very persistent cough, which I would have stifled at all costs if I had I known what would happen next.

We heard the stairs creak as someone came up the stairs. Our door opened, and Dad came into our room. He brought a salve to rub on my chest. I was horrified but felt I could not oppose my dad. I tried to keep myself covered, but he was not satisfied until I was uncovered enough that he could see what he came to see and feel what he wanted to feel. Humiliated and shamed, I *hated* him.

After he had gone downstairs, my sister and I were both furious. Should we dare lock our own dad out? I told her what he had done on that earlier night.

"Why do you keep on going back to him?" my sister fumed. "I am staying as far away from him as I possibly can. He will *not* touch me!"

I had been forgiving toward him before, thinking that he didn't mean to exclude me. The cruelty -- surely it wasn't against me personally. I always thought that I just needed to try harder, to be nicer to him, and to *make* him notice and appreciate me. I wanted to be needed, wanted, and appreciated for who I was, his daughter. But from that moment, I knew that I must change my stance: "He will NOT touch me again!"

~ A Growing Darkness ~

I watched as he was so pleasant to other people. *Why was he not nice to us?* I had wanted the affirmation, love, and affection that he showed to the girls that worked in our bakery. They could look him in the eyes and share in laughter. I did not like to look into his eyes. We were trash to him. I never felt his love. To him, we just existed -- trash that would never amount to anything.

Time went on, and I kept my distance, Dad never inappropriately touched me again. There was a hardness growing in my heart. I quit desiring a relationship with my father and kept my distance as the hardness in my heart grew. With each abuse done to the family, I hated him more. The "*wall*" grew thicker as my heart grew harder.

"You bunch of dirty pigs!" His loud, angry screaming was a constant darkness during our time at home, and it continued to grow. He was ridiculous with his accusations and blaming, especially toward my mother. There was no way that she could be responsible for all that he said was *her fault*. Even a chair would be blamed. If he stubbed his toe, there would be an angry outburst, "That stupid chair!"

The older I got, the more I hated him. I wanted to hurt him. I even wished he would die. He continually said that we would never amount to anything. Without wanting to or realizing it, I embraced some of his words as truth and felt very inferior -- *we were trash.*

~ Forgive Us Our Debts ~

When I was eight years old and in the second grade, I read a small booklet filled with salvation verses from the Bible. On the last page was a message to the reader: "If you have read these verses and believe that Jesus Christ is the Son of God and that He died and shed His blood for the forgiveness of your sins, pray this prayer." I was alone in the house, so I knelt by the couch, and following the prayer on the last page, I gave my heart to Jesus. It had a space to sign my name and write the date, which I did. I kept that little red book with my treasured belongings for a long time.

Eventually, I lost it, but I know that I meant it and felt happy to have done it.

By the time I was fourteen, I was through the eighth grade and out of school. The seriousness of living right in God's eyes and serving Him was growing in me. The anger and hatred bothered me. Even when I was very young, I knew that it was wrong to hate. I also knew that I did not want to move toward forgiveness; hating felt better. I had put up a wall between us, and that wall was more comfortable and felt safer. If I forgave, I feared where that would put me. I liked the distance; it felt safe, but it bothered me.

I prayed the Lord's Prayer, "And forgive our debts as we also have forgiven our debtors" (Matthew 6:12). But I *hadn't* forgiven, so I decided to skip that part. The wall grew thicker.

Mom often told us, "It is not on *our* record (in Heaven) what someone *else* does. We will answer for the deeds that we have done." Over the years, that helped me as I worked my way toward forgiving him. She told us that we are responsible for what *we* do. If *we* respond in anger or in a way that is wrong – *that* goes on *our* record. "Two wrongs never make a right," she often said.

The Lord is gracious in not showing us all our sin at one time. However, He was continuing to convict me about my unforgiving heart.

When Dad beat my brother or one of my other siblings, I wished someone would BEAT HIM -- beat him within an inch of his life! Now God was saying in His Word to forgive. I read the words in The Lord's Prayer, and the words played in my head over and over: "For if you forgive other people when they sin against you, your heavenly Father will also forgive you" (Matthew 6:14). That first part was good, but when I came to the next verse, "But if you do not forgive…." Oh dear! That's me. I had not forgiven. I felt the conviction. I knew that the sin of not forgiving him was darkness. Light and darkness cannot mix. There was no getting around it. I had let Satan's darkness have a place in my heart. "... Your Father will not forgive your sins." I knew I had sins.

I knew *I* wanted the forgiveness of my Heavenly Father.

I began to *want* to forgive. I longed to let it go and be free. I wanted to know and feel the light of His presence and His love living freely in my heart. Choosing forgiveness was hard in the beginning. It meant I needed to let go.

I read, "And when you stand praying, if you hold anything against anyone, forgive them, so that your Father in heaven may forgive you your sins" (Mark 11:25).

I could see I had no choice.

"Okay, God, I want to forgive him." That was the start, but the next time the injustice happened, I found the hate and anger coming back again. It happened again and again. I wrestled again and again.

"Then Peter came to Jesus and asked, 'Lord, how many times shall I forgive my brother or sister who sins against me? Up to seven?" (Matthew 18:21).

Jesus answered, "Not seven times," but "seventy times seven" (KJV Matthew 18:22). In other words, He could have said, "Countless times."

As time passed, I began to feel some victory in the forgiveness battle. I didn't let the angry feelings stay as long. I turned to my Heavenly Father in prayer, asking for help. He is always so faithful, ready to help when we ask. "'You will seek me and find me when you seek me with all your heart. I will be found by you,' declares the Lord" (Jeremiah 29:13-14a).

He helped me see my own need for forgiveness and the great price that was paid for me. The battle was real, and it was not easy. Bit by bit, I grew stronger in this battle. I knew I had victory when I no longer felt the desire to punish him or to wish that somebody else would. I let go of the feelings of revenge, *to make him pay*. Vengeance was not mine to handle, and thankfully so. I just gave it to God. Over time, He replaced the unforgiving spirit with compassion as I let go of the bitterness. I then was able to see some of my dad's frustrations and felt sorry for him.

Years later, I heard a preacher say, "Unforgiveness is like drinking poison and hoping the other will die." No one is hurt more than the person who holds onto hate.

Chapter 9

AMISH YOUTH

I joined the youth group when I was 16.
Besides weekly Sunday night hymn singing, the
youth group had regular activities. Many times we
would have a work bee followed by food and a
game, often volleyball in the summer. One of our
summertime work bee activities that I remember was
a yard raking. A new house was built, and the yard
needed to be seeded for grass. There were many
rocks to be picked up, and we each brought a garden
rake and got the yard ready in a few hours.

~ Box Social ~

One summer evening soon after I had turned
16, the youth had a box social. Usually, the box
social was used as a fundraiser. The girls each
prepared a lunch and put it into a box and placed it
on a table. The boxes were to be auctioned, and a
boy would buy a lunch and then eat it with the girl

who prepared it. This particular evening we weren't going to have the auction part.

Someone had encouraged me to wrap my box in colored newspaper comics. I had only been in the youth group for about two or three months and was a bit reluctant to do it.

When my older brother and sister and I arrived, my sister and I carried our boxes in and placed them on a large table where many beautifully decorated boxes were already placed. Most of the girls' boxes were wrapped in white paper. Some had ribbons, and nearly all had a beautiful, freshly picked, flower bouquet on top. My heart sank. What a mistake to have wrapped my box with newspaper comics! I felt so embarrassed as I placed my box on that table.

Nervously, I waited as the clock ticked to the time appointed to start. Would anyone dare pick the odd box? The boys got to come up one at a time to pick a box, starting with the oldest. As the oldest boy walked to the table, he took his time, picking up one then another. He was a fun-loving, joking type, and was attracted to the comics box. Finally, he surprised everybody as he put back a very pretty box and chose mine!

I had pictured mine being left on the table with a handful of extra girls who didn't get chosen. Suddenly, the picture changed to it being chosen first! As the boxes were chosen, the girl who packed it came forward, and the couple went to the lawn where we all gathered to eat our picnic together. My guy was probably six to eight years older than I and had a girlfriend in another state. After the initial shyness wore off, we enjoyed the night.

~ Corn Husking ~

The Amish farmers husked their corn by hand. One time the youth group helped a needy family who was struggling. Several teams and wagons entered the cornfield one afternoon. There were four people on the wagon that I was on. The two boys took the rows farthest from the wagon, and the two girls took the rows nearest. With jolly bantering and friendly competition, the race was on. The sun had set by the time we finished. What would have taken the farmer weeks to finish alone was all done in one enjoyable afternoon. We shared a hearty meal at the farmhouse before heading home.

~ Mystery Dinners ~

A fun meal we sometimes enjoyed was a Mystery Dinner. The host prepared a meal for the youth and served it with a menu, like a restaurant. All the items of the meal were on the menu with strange "mystery" names. Usually, the name of the food was a hint of what it was, such as corn may be named "Chicken Pellets." They tried to have unguessable items, for instance, by coloring the mashed potatoes pink and calling it "Pink Cloud."

The meal was served in three or four servings. The items marked with "1" were in the first serving. Items marked as "2" were the second serving, and so on. Our drink, napkin, silverware, dessert, and the main course were all on the menu, but each had a mystery name. Sometimes food was served, but the spoon or fork wouldn't come till a later serving. Some got their dessert first.

Sometimes this meal was done around Christmastime, and the food names were Christmassy. The fork may be called "Shepherd's Staff;" the napkin "Swaddling Cloth," etc. Another time it was done in February with "Sweetheart" food names.

~ Skating ~

Frigid winter nights provided skating parties, not only for our youth group, but for all ages on the pond. After work and chores, several of the youth group gathered together after dark with lanterns for fun together on the ice. Many times snow had to be scraped off. I remember a night when there was a lot of snow, so the boys didn't clear it all off but made curvy paths, and a vigorous game of tag was played. Usually, there was some light from a fire on the bank, where hot chocolate and snacks were served.

~ Describe ~

Also in the wintertime, we had a variety of indoor games and activities. Sometimes we played Describe. We each wrote our name on a piece of paper. All the papers were placed in a basket and mixed by tossing; then we all drew one. If we drew our own name it had to be put back, and we drew again. The name we drew was the person we described. The person who guessed the most correctly was the winner.

One time we were playing this game, and I was pleasantly pleased with the boy's name I had drawn. I was starting to have an attraction to this boy and did my very best to give him a great description.

To my embarrassment, the reader reading the description I had written, pointed out that the describer had forgotten to put the letter "r" in the word "shirt." I described in my clue the color of shirt he was wearing that night. I wished the reader would gloss over my mistake. Instead, it was exaggerated, and everybody laughed. It was consoling that at least nobody knew who made the mistake.

~ Walk-a-Mile ~

When I was 18, a new schoolhouse was built, and the hardwood floor needed sanding. The youth group was invited for a "sanding" event. After the work, we played "Walk-a-Mile." It was dark, and we took a walk on the road. The boys and girls paired up and held hands as they walked in a long "train" two by two along the side of the road. The boys would trade the girl they walked with every five minutes or so and kept circulating throughout the entire walk.

There were always more girls than boys. Sometimes, when the boys and girls would pair up, I found myself in the "leftover girl group." However, this night a boy came back to the extra girl group, looking for a certain one. I remember telling the girl with me, "Go ahead. You're probably the one he's looking for." To my surprise, he asked for me! Wow! This *boy* later became my husband. That was the first time he openly showed any special interest in me, and we enjoyed our walk that night.

Chapter 10

A CHANGE OF MIND

I had resolved in my heart that I would *never* get married. "It's not worth it," I thought. Gradually, my mind adjusted to positive thoughts about marriage the summer I was 17. I worked for our Amish neighbors and totally enjoyed the happy farm life.

The harmony I saw in their home was so different from mine. Their marriage was an example of teamwork to me, and the possibility of a nice marriage was forming in my mind.

The mornings at their home started early, but I enjoyed helping milk the cows and eating a good breakfast at the start of each new day.

One evening, I asked if there was something I could do to help in the kitchen as the mother was bustling about. "If you can just entertain the children, it would be a help to me," she answered. I was happy to do it and so were the children. We had a great time, and many evenings it was my *job* to play with the children.

~ "Rum Shpringa" ~

Amish parents often had concerns for their children in the larger communities. The youth would stray from the *Ordnung*. Many of them would "sow their wild oats." This time is often referred to as *Rum Shpringa*[1] (running around), a time in the teenage years when they got cars, dressed worldly, etc. Parents disapproved and hoped that this would only last for a short period of time. They expected that the strays would come back, get married, and settle down. In our small community, we didn't have the *Rum Shpringa*.

To protect their youth, a family may relocate to a new community to avoid the *Rum Shpringa*. It is very common for a family to move to another

---

[1] Editor's Note: Because Pennsylvania Dutch is usually not a written dialect, some of the spellings may vary. For the purpose of this book, we chose a spelling that shows the variation of pronunciation in Rebecca's community.

community when they do not agree with a part of the *Ordnung.* A small group may go off and start a new community, often taking the same "recipe" and hoping for a new or different "soup."

When I was 14, a new Amish family who wanted a better environment for their young, teenage children moved from a larger community to be our neighbors. Until they moved in, we were not used to seeing a buggy go past our house because we lived the farthest west in our community.

One summer evening, I rode Billy to the new neighbors' house with a message from my parents. Ivan, their oldest son, was in the meadow making his way toward the barn. A cat jumped on a fence post to sit, lick her paws, and clean her face. I watched from the back of my pony as Ivan fixed his eyes on the cat and crept up to her. *Would he be mean to her? Would he pull her tail?*

He got closer to the cat, but she did not notice him. He got right to her and reached out with both hands, closing in on her with a "Boo!"

The cat was startled for a split-second, but when she saw him she instantly relaxed, as though to say, "Ah, it's *you!*" She purred and arched her back for the petting she received.

Well, now that was nice, I thought. I could tell that the cat trusted him. My mom told us, "As a man treats his animals, is likely how he will also treat his wife."

Around seven years later I married that boy.

~ Dating ~

Dating would take place at the girl's home on Sunday nights. After the Youth Hymn Singing, a boy would take his date to her home, and they would spend time visiting in her bedroom upstairs.

When I was 18, and I started having some thoughts of a boy bringing me home from the singing, I realized my room was not ready. All the other dating-age girls had a two-seat couch in their rooms for their dates.

Our house was remodeled in my early teens, and I was able to move from sharing a room with my sister to having a room of my own. It was a tiny room with two windows, side by side, facing south. The space for my bed along the west wall to the little closet door was five feet. I had a bed frame built to fit those five feet and placed a piece of foam rubber on top for my mattress. We girls helped Mom make a quilt to fit my bed, as it was such an in-between size. Nothing regular would fit.

My room was too small to add a couch, even if the couch was small enough for only two. Many of the other girls had an old car seat fixed in a frame to stand on her bedroom floor. It would be covered with a blanket and held two or three people comfortably. I asked my brother Levi if he could get me a car seat BACK only, which he did. Then I wrapped two bricks in tinfoil and placed them on the floor under the front legs of my little bed, for a slant in the seat. The car seat back was on top of my bed along the wall. Then I draped a blanket over the whole thing, and "wa-lah!" -- there was my seat. During the week, the bricks were under my bed, and the car seat back took up nearly half of my closet.

One Sunday afternoon soon after my "seat" preparations were made, Ivan's sister Clara whispered in my ear, "Would you be willing to have Ivan for a date tonight?" It was typical for a boy to have his sister ask his girl for him. Rarely, did the boy ask the girl himself. They would "grapevine" through siblings or best friends. Sometimes, the date was arranged through the mail. The girl could accept or reject the date.

I was pleased to accept the date with Ivan. All smiles, I squeezed her hand.

A date was kept secret from the youth group, as was the tradition. Only in the following week would the rumors float around about who had a date with whom.

The youth from both districts gathered weekly for Sunday night singings. The week following my first date, as we were getting our bonnets and shawls to go home, I heard the whispers of two girls discussing who had a date with whom, and my ears perked when I heard my name.

"Did you know that Rebecca had a date?"

"She did! WHO?"

"Ivan," said the first.

"Oh, *just him*." the second answered.

To them, I knew that I was *just her,* and my date was *just him.*

I began to look forward to every three or four weeks having another date. We would arrive at my home between nine and ten o'clock. While he unhitched the horse and took her to the barn, I hurried to the house and started to heat the water for tea. Ivan liked hot tea, especially in the winter. The tea was ready when he came into the kitchen. We carried the tea pitcher, two cups, and a plate of cookies that I had made the day before and headed up the stairs to my little room.

We kept our voices low because others in the house were sleeping as we talked and laughed until midnight when he would leave to go home. One favorite story that Ivan shared, happened on a Saturday morning when both of his parents were gone. His sister Freida was cleaning in her upstairs bedroom. For some reason, there was a hook on the outside of her bedroom door. Ivan decided to play a trick on her and reached out and quietly dropped the hook into the eye. Frieda heard the click and tried to open the door; sure enough, it was latched.

"Let me out!" she ordered as she pounded on the door from the inside. He knew he was in trouble now. He surveyed the distance and came up with a plan for the quickest escape. There were only a few steps to the front door at the bottom of the stairs.

The "temperature" was rising from behind the locked door, and he knew he must open it and move quickly. He unlatched it and took off down the steps at top speed, his sister in hot pursuit, broom in hand.

On the porch outside, a neighbor stood ready to knock just as the door flew open! Ivan let his sister stay and face the neighbor while he kept on running.

In his family, when the women needed to go somewhere, he or his dad would get the horse ready for them. Not so in my family. We had to get our own horse ready. Ivan took care of his sisters, one older and one younger. Many times, his sisters rode with us to or from the singings because they depended on their brother for transportation.

I told my mom that I wished that it could be the two of us alone. "One day that 'caring for' will be yours. You be thankful that he is a caring person," Mom encouraged me. I cherished the thought of that "love and care" being mine one day as our friendship grew.

Some beautiful, moonlit summer nights, we would walk on our quiet gravel road hand in hand. One summer night, it was stuffy, and no breeze came through the windows. We left the house and went to check out the whimpering noise coming from the barn. Our dog, Trixie, had new puppies, and one had fallen out of the box and couldn't get back in. We helped it back in, and Trixie promptly got in and nursed her litter. Then we went to Judy, Ivan's horse, and offered her some more hay. She stepped impatiently from side to side then pawed with a front foot, telling her master she was ready to go home. It wasn't midnight yet, so we sat in his buggy. The minutes flew by, and all too soon our time together was over.

For the first year or so, we dated every three or four weeks. We never kissed until we were "steady," which I imagine is the equivalent of "engaged" in the English world. The closest thing to a proposal in our dating was when he asked me to be his "steady." That meant we would not date anyone else, and we would see each other every Sunday night. We were officially a "couple" in the community.

Sometime after we were "steady," Ivan suggested that we start our night together by reading the Bible. I remember the text he picked the first night, Genesis 24. It tells the story of Abraham sending his servant to get Rebekah for a wife for his son, Isaac.

We dated for three years. I felt he took his "good ol' time" getting around to talking about marriage. I felt ready for marriage at twenty and wished he were too. I was "in prison" at home, working for my parents until I was 21. Until we were

21, we handed our earnings to our parents. *If I could get married at twenty, I could get out sooner*, I thought.

He was happy in his home and in no hurry to leave. He was a year older than I, and when he turned 21, he began to keep the money he made. He joined a carpentry crew when he was 18 years old. All but 10 percent of his earnings went to his parents. After he was 21, he paid 10 percent to his parents for rent and continued to live with them until we were married.

Chapter 11

OUR WEDDING

An Amish wedding is traditionally at the bride's home. Ours was in the top story of the barn, where everything was moved out and cleaned. Fresh hay covered the barn floor, and the benches were set.

I was aware of the white bride's dress of the English. I thought it would be wonderful, so would wedding pictures. They were both out of the question for me. We were not allowed to have pictures, so we have no pictures from the day that we got married. I made my wedding cake but was not allowed to have colored icing or flowers on it. It was large, round and had four layers frosted with white icing.

I made my wedding dress with the same pattern that I used for all of my dresses. Everyone wants a special dress for their special day. The only thing special about mine was that it was new. It was dark blue which was my only option according to the *Ordnung*. I had a white cape and apron, the same as I would normally wear to church. In our community the girls' head coverings were black, and the married women wore white. Some communities let the bride and her maids wear white after the ceremony for the rest of the day. I remember asking one of the older women who came to help with the preparations if I could do this. The answer was "That's not how we do it here," which meant, "No."

Amish weddings are announced to the church several weeks before the actual planned date. It is supposed to be a surprise to the community. Only the family and a few close friends know this "secret" date ahead of the announcement. All my plans and preparations were in secret until after my wedding was announced, then we had a few weeks to prepare openly. My sister and I got married in the same week, two days apart. If I had it to do over, I would choose to have both on the same day. We could have saved so much, in so many ways. At the time, I wanted my own day.

The problems at home escalated when we closed the bakery down for the weddings. For the previous five to six years, we older children ran the bakery while Dad spent his days out on the road with a hired driver. He delivered cereal and bought supplies. I don't know where he went or what else he did, but things were so much more peaceful at home when he was not there.

Dad was so angry these days. We never argued with him, but usually remained silent. Our respect for him was gone. He had lost emotional contact with his family. The method that he had chosen for controlling us had not worked.

He grumbled, protesting the interruption that these "funerals" were causing in his life. That was what he called our weddings. We could do nothing but continue with our plans and preparations.

Once, from the window of my room upstairs, I even heard him crying. *Is he feeling sorry for himself?* Another day he carried a gun around. We were so fearful of what he might do with the gun.

When he left it outside the bedroom door at the end of the day, we hid it.

The weddings had been announced, and we only had a few weeks with much preparation still needing to be done. I was concerned about doing what was "right" in God's sight. This time of preparing for the weddings was intensely busy and difficult because of my dad's actions.

One night I had a dream which reminded me of Mom's words as she taught us that we are not responsible for another man's actions. What we *are* responsible for is our response and our own actions. We will be rewarded for what *we* have done "...and they will each be rewarded according to their own labor" (1 Corinthians 3:8).

By experiencing the dream, I knew that God knew our situation and was with us. My duty through this all was to stay right with Him, not letting the evil around me poison me. God does not take us out of all our trouble, but He is with us as we go through it. "But he knows the way that I take; when he has tested me, I will come forth as gold"

(Job 23:10). God wants us to be overcomers. "I have told you these things, so that in me you may have peace. In this world you will have trouble. But take heart! I have overcome the world" (John 16:33).

Our wedding day turned out to be beautiful. When we set the date for August, I had concerns about it being uncomfortably warm. The day dawned cool in the morning with blue skies and fluffy white clouds appearing in the afternoon. After the seating of our 200 guests, the service began at 9 AM, the same as a regular church service and ended at noon.

Meanwhile, several ladies including my aunts and my mom were in the bakery as it buzzed with the preparation of food. The table waiters were getting their instructions and helping where needed. We had chosen around ten unmarried couples who were from the youth group of our community and our cousins from out-of-state.

There were six people in our wedding party, as was traditional. We were given the special privilege of having chairs instead of benches. The bride has a girl on each side of her, and the groom has a boy on each side of him. The wedding party is seated in the center of the congregation, the three boys on the men's side and the three girls on the women's side, facing each other.

Nearing the noon hour, all the cooks and table waiters left their work and filed into the barn to witness the actual exchange of our vows. After they were all settled, my heartbeat quickened when the bishop turned to us and said, "If you still feel like you did this morning, you may rise and come forward." I have never known of a couple that changed their minds.

The congregation stood as he read a prayer from the prayer book; then all were seated except the wedding party. The bishop placed our hands together and put his over ours to speak the vows, "... to have and to hold, from this day forward, for better, for worse, for richer, for poorer, in sickness and in health, to love and to cherish, until death do us part."

The bishop pronounced us husband and wife. We returned to our seats, and the six of us sat down together. The workers returned to the task of preparing the feast as the closing song, a traditional song used at every wedding, was sung. After the song, the six of us stood and left the barn first. Next, the congregation was excused.

The feast was ready, and tables were set in the house. We had china dishes and serving bowls for the tables, no paper plates and plasticware. Some of it was borrowed from neighbors.

We had fried chicken, dressing, mixed vegetables, mashed potatoes, and gravy. For dessert we had date pudding, which is broken pieces of date cake layered with sliced bananas, caramel sauce, and whipped topping and served in glass bowls. We had cake with Mom's caramel icing, pie, and ice cream. I can't remember which were served at noon and which were served for supper, but we had abundant, delicious feasts.

Our table waiters served the tables, washed the dishes, and then cleaned and reset the tables until all had eaten. There were fewer people for the evening meal, which was mainly for relatives, many of which were from out-of-state.

The wedding evening was always special for the youth. The boys chose a partner to sit with at the table. Many relationships started at someone's wedding and resulted in marriage. That night, our young married cousins were the table waiters for all the guests. After the meal, the youth sang for an hour.

I was a happy bride. One of my sisters told me that she overheard someone say, "She looks so serious." They didn't know my home-life and the issues that my siblings and I faced, especially in the weeks leading up to the wedding. But I got a good man. I love the fact that I can put my feet on his side of the bed even when they are very cold, and he welcomes me to get warm.

There was no honeymoon. The first night we slept on a mattress on the floor of my very tiny bedroom. The next day we helped clean up and put things in order for my sister's wedding.

Our wedding gifts and my few belongings were loaded onto a steel-wheeled farm wagon pulled by two horses. We headed off to our new home and future. My husband had used all his savings for a downpayment on an old farmhouse with ten acres. We started with very little money, and we barely scraped by financially. My dreams of helping with an income for a few years before we had children were short-lived. In a few weeks we were expecting, not one baby, but two! We ate a lot of soup those first years, but we were happy.

CHAPTER 12

WHY WE LEFT

We had intended to spend the rest of our lives in the Amish community. The way of life was good. Some folks long for modern conveniences, and they "crowd the fence." We did not.

We did have a problem with the church rules and discipline. The keeping of the *Ordnung* was made as important as the Bible. At times, the emphasis on maintaining the *Ordnung* seemed even more important than the Bible. Our responsibility to the bishop was emphasized more than our relationship to God.

Twice a year communion was served, and things had to be in order according to the church's man-made *Ordnung.* The punishment for not having things in order meant a member could not participate in communion.

For instance, if a farmer had recently bought machinery with air tires, which weren't allowed, he had a certain amount of time to get the tires changed to rubber or steel. If he didn't get them changed in the allowed time, then he couldn't participate in communion. Rules had to be kept to take communion.

Many of the rules were based on outward appearances, striving to make us all look alike and act alike. "Like a Pepsi Cola machine," some outsider said. "They all come out the same. They look alike, smell alike, taste alike."

I believe the original purpose was for our *unity*, but I think it became *uniformity*. That's not how God made us. He made us all different, and He did it on purpose! Why should we try and make people all the same? God made us different in looks, tastes, and talents. The strength of one fills the weakness of another, making the body of Christ complete.

I felt that church discipline also focused on outward appearance. This focus lead members to critically inspect each other, making sure that everyone was in order. It also lead to another result:

members felt that they could get by with things if they were not caught. We were trying to please the bishop instead of being accountable to God, Who sees in secret. A person can have sin in his heart, hidden from the human eye, but God sees the heart and knows all the hidden issues. A good passage that shows that we cannot hide from God is Psalms 139:1-12.

Many things began to stir a hunger in us for a more spiritual connection with God. We wanted to know Him more. We wanted a relationship with Him, and we longed for more teaching from His Word.

"One can just read too much Bible," one of the older women in church said when she heard that some had left the Amish church. Their testimony for leaving was that they were reading the Bible; its teaching lead to God and His truth, which lead them to leave the Amish. Her remedy was *not to read the Bible so much.*

Rarely did an Amish person engage in an open conversation about God and the Bible. We were newly married, and we knew a few members that were fairly open to talking about spiritual things. Word got around that there was a meeting in a town an hour away. Two Romanian women were going to give their testimonies about their lives in prison because they were Christians. A small group of us were open to go and hear them. We hired a driver with a van and split the cost of the trip. We knew that we could get in trouble with the church for going to a non-Amish meeting.

One of the Romanian ladies told how she was given the punishment of cleaning the prison toilet. She was not given any shovel or scoop; she had to do it with her bare hands. She began to do it with one hand and to hold her nose with the other. The guard didn't allow this. He ordered her to use both hands.

They talked about the food if one can call it food. I don't remember all of the facts, but that it was awful. They ate bread crusts and watery soup. One time, the speaker said she was very hungry for an apple. She prayed and asked God for one. Later, she asked the guard if it would be possible for her to get an apple. He eventually brought one. They were so excited and happy to receive it! When they opened the bag, there was a brown, rotten apple.

"But," she said, "it turned out to be a blessing anyway. We didn't have solid food for such a long time, and our teeth were in bad condition. We could probably not have bitten into it." She said that they ate the rotten apple, and it was so sweet and one of the most delicious things that they had in a long time.

As they spoke, we were deeply moved. They spoke of a God that answered prayers. God was answering prayer *today*, not just back in Abraham's day. God was very much alive in their testimony *today*.

Sadly, the Amish church did not approve of any of its members going to meetings like these. Neither did they approve of a man that later became our good friend, Arthur Leis. His influence would help to change our lives.

We heard of Arthur through some customers we met in our bulk food store. We had the store in the same building as the bakery. We sold a variety of bulk food items, meat, and cheese, along with the bread and cereal we made in the bakery.

The Beoughers were customers in our store. George and Kathy had children our age, and we became good friends. Their daughter, Martha, was my age and size so she could wear my Amish clothes. We dressed her in the Amish attire and took her with us to the Youth Hymn Singing. She looked totally Amish, and some of our friends spoke to her in the Amish language, which she, of course, could not understand. The picture on the front cover of this book is Martha wearing my clothes. I don't have any photographs of myself as we were not allowed to have any.

Kathy Beougher was instrumental in helping my mom to find comfort and strength in God and to open His Word. By her own testimony, she shared how God provided for them in some of their most difficult times.

One night the Beoughers had a missionary at their church, and they invited my parents to hear him. The missionary was Arthur Leis. He was from Canada and in his late 50s. He explained why he became a missionary. He experienced an "open vision." I had never heard of such a thing. One night, in 1952, he was in his living room, while his wife was in the kitchen. He was reading the book *Jungle Doctor* by Paul White and looking at a picture of a little African boy. He said that suddenly, the little "fella" was standing at his knee, and he reached out his hand, touching the top of the boy's head. Then, it was as if the wall were gone, and he saw several Africans. They were talking to him, begging, "Come and live among us. You belong here."

He replied that he couldn't come. "I have no money. I don't have an education."

He made excuses, and they nodded and said, "We will wait for you." As they went away, another group came, also asking him to come and help them. He saw a number of tribes and groups, each asking him to come and then saying, "We will wait for you."

His wife came in from the kitchen and asked, "Who are you talking to?"

With tears in his eyes, he answered, "These people. They are asking me to come." She couldn't see anyone.

In time he did go to each of the tribes he saw in his vision. He lived among the people for most of 40 years. He told us many stories and spoke of the miracles that God had done in the years he spent in Africa. His book is being written at the time of this writing.

He is now a white-haired man, walking with a cane. We went to visit him last summer, and I asked him to tell me again some of the stories he had told us years ago. He did, in his soft voice with tears in his eyes. He remembered "the dealing of God in his life."

He shared a beautiful truth during that visit that I believe is applicable for all of us in some area of our lives: "At the time," he said, "I didn't know why God wanted it done the way He told me, but now looking back I can see. I understand it now." I believe that one day we too will be able to see the "whys" we can't see now.

To trust and obey is what God wants us to do, as we walk by faith. Someone has said that hope is faith in the future. Faith helps you to live in that space between what you understand and what you don't.

Arthur's stories also spoke of an active God who was working *now* in our lives. I wanted more of this, more of God! Our Amish church was busy keeping its members in the *Ordnung*. I began to see the big chasm between these two worlds.

The Amish wanted us to know that they had all the spirituality that we needed and there was no need to look beyond what they offered. Problems, like we had at home when I was growing up, were admonished, but they offered no constructive aid or teaching to help bring hope and correction. The deacon of the church admitted that the leaders knew

Dad told them untruths, but it seemed that they had no power to deal with our family's trouble.

The Amish never talked about a relationship with God. They did not teach assurance of salvation. The Amish church taught us that we could only *hope* for our salvation. One preacher gave the example of rolling a wheel down a hill. If it landed on one side, our destiny was Hell; if it landed on the other side, it was Heaven. "We *hope* it will land on the side of Heaven." They feel that the good works will help tilt the wheel on the side of Heaven. It was like flipping a coin!

Arthur Leis attended our wedding. For a wedding gift, he said he would take us on a free trip to his home in Canada and that we could stop in at Niagara Falls. In our Amish life, we would need to hire a driver for such a trip; free was appealing. About two years later, true to his promise, we made the trip.

Many things happened to us on our spiritual journey on that trip. Arthur took us to his church in Canada, and we were inspired by the spiritual things we encountered there. Unknown to us, Arthur had arranged the timing of this trip to be on a weekend of revival services. There was a total of three days of services. The first time we walked into that church was on a Friday evening. We were in our Amish clothes and felt out of place. The people in that church were friendly and accepted us as we were. They made us feel at home the best that they could.

We knew and accepted the fact that his church would be much different than our Amish church. We would *tolerate* his church as part of the package and enjoy Niagara Falls on the way home and then our Amish life would go on as it always had.

Though things at that church service were different, we were not able to oppose the teaching we encountered with anything greater than the tradition we knew, our Amish *Ordnung*. They had reasons based on scripture for functioning the way they did. Our spiritual hunger was met, and we were being inspired by the Word of God in a way we never experienced before.

We stopped at Niagara Falls on the way home. Many people there were not used to seeing the Amish. They would turn and look at us, but we were used to it.

When we were on the Maid of the Mist, the boat took us toward the falls. The loudspeaker told us various historical facts, and we soon began to experience the mist. The announcer said that it was a good time to put on our raincoats. Soon everybody was wearing black raincoats.

"They're not staring at us anymore!" my husband observed. I hadn't noticed, but he was exactly right. We were among the "English," and for the first time, we were able to blend in and look normal. I was in my mid-twenties and had never experienced this before.

After we left the falls, we headed toward home. The new things that we had encountered replayed through my thoughts. As familiar landscapes came into view, my thoughts turned back to the Amish life. In the entire church, whom could I talk to about how I felt?

We still had no intentions of leaving the Amish, but my heart was heavy as I looked across the green fields. A heavy feeling of dread weighed on me as I thought about the thing the Amish leaders were concerned about -- keeping their members in the *Ordnung*. I never saw the deadness of it all until after we experienced the spiritual life on this trip. The color seemed to fade; the bright green of the hills and the trees seemed dull.

The closer we got to home, the heavier my thoughts of the Amish life felt. We were taught that we could not break the promise to stay with the Amish when we were baptized into the church. It was taught that it was wrong, and we didn't want to do anything wrong. The fear of being excommunicated was huge. The whole trip was helping to expose our emptiness inside.

CHAPTER 13

A LEAP OF FAITH

We began to consider the options of other churches. We looked at the New Order Amish which allowed more material things and more Bible teaching. We found their practices more godly. That leap seemed doable, but would it solve our problem? We had a friend that had just left the New Order Amish to joined the Beachy Church, a church allowing cars and electricity. He told us about the New Order council meeting, and it sounded much like what we had come from.

It still seemed like a fence, only with a larger fenced-in circle. Naturally, our friend encouraged us not to go to the New Order but to come to where he was, the Beachy Church. That leap was a bit bigger. Our Old Order church would tolerate us leaving them to go to the New Order, and they would not excommunicate us for it. They *would* excommunicate us for going to the *car church*.

Each of the churches that we visited was open to having us leave the more conservative order to join them, but if we thought of going beyond them, it was frowned upon. Each seemed to have an unspoken "we have arrived" mentality. Our Old Order church frowned upon us going to the New Order church. The New Order frowned upon us leaving them to go to the Beachy Church. We soon realized that they were all the same religious system.

I am saddened by the "walls" that divide the various Amish churches which have sprung up in the last 30 years. I can't keep up with all the different "flavors" one can choose from today. The uniformity they practice is not bringing unity. Has their foundation moved off the true foundation? "For no one can lay any foundation other than the one already laid, which is Jesus Christ" (1 Corinthians 3:11).

I see *human control* like an impurity, like a foreign object in the work of God. A wound cannot heal with a splinter buried inside. We humans can *appear* to be good or right to each other, but sooner or later the truth is revealed.

In a hurricane, flooding, or other natural devastation, people lay down their differences. They quit looking at skin colors and backgrounds. All the pecking order is left behind. People reach out to help each other. Jesus is coming back for *one* body, His church. Does it take a disaster before we Christians stand together?

We had some friends from some of these circles that reached out to us to help us in our pursuit of God. They brought their Bibles and came to teach the Word of God to us and to share their testimonies. We were hungry, and their help was an encouragement.

One night as they approached our home for another Bible teaching, they said that they saw a white cloud hovering over the house. They stopped and watched as it formed into the shape of a funnel. They said angels came out of the bottom of it and encircled the entire house.

On other nights the Old Order Amish preachers came, admonishing us not to travel the route we were on. They did not bring their Bibles, and they did not bring us encouragement. They told us fear stories of people who had traveled the road we were on.

"Those people ended up leaving the faith," meaning leaving Amish. They said, "Now they would like to come back, but their children won't come. They are out in the world." Their words were intended to strike fear into our hearts, and it did. We certainly didn't want to go *out into the world.*

We noticed the fear and confusion that occurred when the Amish preachers visited. It was such a contrast to the encouragement we were learning from our Bible studies. We were threatened with excommunication. It was the greatest threat they could hand us. Excommunication implied we were no longer in the fold but on the way to Hell.

When we discussed the differences between our counselors, we noted that the Amish preachers came and laid their big black hats on the table. The others laid their Bibles on the table. After the Amish left, we felt condemnation and fear. After the others left, we were encouraged by God's Word. The question became what were we basing our life decisions on – the Bible or man-made rules?

During this time we met a man who readily spoke of the goodness of God. Bob Bixler's face lit up with the joy of the Lord as he testified of what God was doing in his life. We shared our frustrations of man-made rules and churches steeped-in tradition. We were searching for one which concentrated on a relationship with God.

At one of the last Amish church services we attended, the preacher said in his sermon that he was mowing hay in his field. On one round he noticed that the tracks of his wheel from the previous round had narrowly missed running directly over a bird's nest with little ones in it. "If one of those little birds would have left the safety of the nest," he said, "even just a few inches, it could have been the death of it." We knew his interpretation was *safety came in staying Amish.* We also understood the Bible's teaching that *obedience to God* is our safety.

We knew leaving meant being cut off from family and friends. The Amish have big families with an average of ten children. We knew there would be weddings and funerals where we would be outsiders if we showed up.

We hurt most for my husband's parents. The hardest thing my husband ever did was to tell his parents, "We're not coming back." I stayed with the twins, now two years old, the morning he walked the short distance across the field to his parents' house. His parents and four siblings were seated around the breakfast table. In response to his announcement, his parents both wept.

While my husband was gone, I left the house to feed the chickens and gather the eggs. I heard the sound of an approaching buggy. It was the bishop coming to announce the "work of the church." The vote was unanimous to excommunicate us. We were now to be shunned by all our people.

I wished that my husband was with me as I faced the bishop alone, but he was doing a much harder task alone. The bishop was very brief and to the point. I know it was hard for him as well. We had been good friends over the years.

For the past several months, we had sensed that the excommunication was going to happen. How we dreaded it! Was there no way around it? We had prayed about our decision, and we had counted the cost. To be cut off from the only life we knew and to step into the *English* world was a HUGE Leap of Faith! We knew the truth, and we knew we had acted on it. God spoke to us through His Word.

After the bishop's visit, my husband and I suddenly felt a huge relief and freedom. We were no longer torn between being loyal to the Amish church rules and being loyal to God and the scriptures. We were going to trust Him and walk by faith. When the apostles Peter and John were told not to preach in the name of Jesus, they said, "…which is right in God's eyes: to listen to you, or to Him? You be the judges!" (Acts 4:19).

Bob Bixler invited us to visit his church and offered to pick us up and take us. He went to a nondenominational church. Surely, this must be our answer, *non* denominational! There were eight of us that left the Amish church at the same time: two single adults and three young families with children. We all piled into the back of Bob's small pickup truck that had a cap on it and rode the thirty minutes to New Jerusalem Fellowship. We spent much of the traveling time singing one song after the next.

At the church a small group of friendly people welcomed us. The pastor was an excellent teacher on law and grace and helped us to gain the understanding we needed to transition from the legalistic setting we came from.

A young, married Amish couple did their duty as a good "builder of the church" to come for a visit around the time of our excommunication. They were there for one reason: to urge us to rethink our decision and return to the fold. I told the young wife that in many ways it would be so much easier just to forget it all and stay.

"Yeah, I can imagine it would be much easier to hop in your car to go someplace than to get your horse ready to go," she said. Was this sarcasm? I knew that she only saw the natural side of it. Did she even know there was a spiritual side?

In our Amish life, we did not need to have our own convictions. The rules were set before us, and the bishop made the final decisions. Yet the Amish bishop will not be standing before God for our actions. We will give account for the choices that we made. Through the whole time that we were taking that leap of faith, we always had a thread of Light and Life leading us.

At times a sadness enveloped me when I thought about the things I had lost: my church, my relatives, and the only world I ever knew. One side of me wanted just to let go and slide back into familiarity, but the other side of me fought on principle.

It was very hard for me to sell Trudy, our faithful horse. I loved that beautiful horse, but we could not afford to keep her. I thought back to how I would hitch her to the buggy and put the twins in a banana box lined with a soft blanket. It fit perfectly on the floor by my feet. Off we would go, often to see my mom a few miles away. Many things in my life were changing, and it would never be the same again.

New Jerusalem Fellowship is where we went every Sunday after the Amish church excommunicated us. The pastor and his wife started coming to our house on Wednesdays for Bible teaching, and they helped us with getting our driver's licenses. For a short time, Bob Bixler continued to pick us up until we got our own vehicles. We were in our mid-twenties when we made this Leap of Faith and have not regretted one day of it.

CHAPTER 14

MOM FINDS A NEW LIFE

There was still much trouble in my parents'
home. The more we had reached out for help from
the church leadership, the more despair there was on
our part. The last time Mom went for help, they told
her to go home and be quiet.

As time went on, my parents continued to
draw further apart. To divorce literally was not
permissible. One of their many issues was their
sleeping arrangements. Finally, Mom got two single
beds and set them up side by side. Now he wouldn't
feel it when she moved. Sometimes her body would
jerk as she relaxed enough to fall asleep. When this
happened, he would kick her legs and tell her to quit
bothering his sleep.

Mom came home one day, and her bed was
gone. She had no idea why or what had happened, so
she slept in an extra bed in an upstairs room. Around
two months later her bed was returned.

"So that's where my bed went!" my mom said to the lady from their church who brought it back.

"Huh! What do you mean?" she asked, truly surprised. "That was *your* bed?"

"I slept in it every night," Mom answered.

"Your husband told us, 'We've got an extra bed you can have. No one is using it.'"

I recently heard a preacher on the radio speaking about God's plan for the love that a man should have for his wife. He quoted from Ephesians, "Husbands, love your wives, just as Christ loved the church and gave himself up for her" (5:25). He went on to explain that through this love, the wife can fully become what God designed her to be. He also said that some men feel threatened with any abilities, development, or gifts that their wives may have. The domineering husband may try to stifle his wife in every way that he can. A man like this will try to shut his wife down to the point where she begins to doubt her own personal value, he explained.

Sadly, that describes what was happening in our home. Jesus said, "...whoever wants to become great among you must be your servant, and whoever wants to be first must be slave of all. For even the Son of Man did not come to be served, but to serve, and to give his life as a ransom for many" (Mark 10:43 - 45).

Jesus was an example of serving. Unfortunately, it seems, Dad never learned the truth of serving. We kept seeing him putting others down, especially his spouse, in order that he would be first, lifted up, or important. He kept lifting himself up, trying to *make it big* in life by his own strength. The world does many things opposite of Jesus who says, "Give, and you shall receive." The world says, "Get for yourself, and get more."

Life in that Amish community became impossible for my mom. Three of my siblings were now married, and we all left that Amish church at the same time and for the same reason. The Amish leaders now concentrated on making sure that Mom didn't mess-up the rules concerning our excommunication. She must keep the *Meidung* (shunning). She could not eat or ride with us or accept anything from us.

They also did not want to see our cars parked in plain sight when we came home. Then when we parked in the shed and pulled the door shut, they said we were hiding our cars.

After most of us older children were out of the house, my parents continued to drift apart. Mom stayed in the home and took care of the house, yard, and garden. She had no support from Dad or the church. Finally, she gave up on the Amish, and the church excommunicated her. She got a job caring for the elderly. She rode with the neighbor lady who also worked at the same place. The times when they were not working at the same hours, we children took her, brought her home, or both.

My sister bought her a car and handed her the keys saying, "Here, now you can take yourself to work!" She did. She got another job, paid for the car, and bought a better one. She took my youngest sister, who was the only one still at home, and attended the Apostolic church in town for the next ten years.

During this time when Mom was not Amish, she still lived at home. She had my brothers put electricity and a phone in the house. She did well with her jobs and was loved by the people she worked for. She also used her wages to update the upstairs with wallpaper and paint.

Dad lived his separate life and remained in the Amish church. The church did not allow phones in the house, and he needed one for his business. He got permission from the neighbors and put a phone in a booth on the opposite side of the road on the neighbors' land. I am sure it was a huge relief to the patient English neighbors who had been letting him come into their house daily to do his phone business.

One day the phone rang, and Dad ran across the road to answer it. Mom happened to pick up the extension in the house at the exact same time that he did and heard the conversation without Dad knowing it. The man on the other end was talking with my dad about her, so she listened. She heard Dad say,

"I've tried to take her down, but I can't. She's too strong for me."

Meanwhile, my brother Paul was having severe PTSD (post-traumatic stress disorder) and could hardly cope with life. He went to a home for troubled boys in Michigan which was run by Amish. In order to get to the facts of their coping problems, the boys were required to talk openly about their lives, spilling all the nasty details. As Paul told the leader about his home life, the leader said, "I don't believe what you are telling me, but if it is true, how can your mom survive?"

"She can't," Paul told him. "That is why she left the Amish, not because she wanted to, but there was nothing else left to do."

"Would she like to come back?" the leader of the home asked.

"She would desire to live Amish, but not there. Not like it was." Then he gave Paul the permission to call Mom and extend an offer for her to come to the home for a safe place to live.

The home offered to let her come on a trial basis for two weeks. She accepted and drove the five-hour trip alone to the Amish facility and stayed the two weeks. After the two weeks, she decided to live there and drove back home to put her things in order. It took around two months to quit her jobs, sell her car, and get things in order at home to leave. My youngest brother took her back to the home in Michigan, and Mom went through the program for a year and a half.

Through that home, the offer was made to help my mom come back to the Amish life in a different setting. That leader of the home was the only Amish person that reached out to help my mom return. He asked her to find a church she would like to become a member of, and he would be the middleman to help her do it.

A year later the home asked her to return as an assistant house parent. She accepted the offer and enjoyed it and was liked by those in the home. One day while Mom was working, I was there for a visit and witnessed an act I haven't forgotten. Everybody was gathering for breakfast, and I noticed a boy that seemed to be wearing a don't-look-at-me face. He stopped at a small mirror hanging on the wall, pulled a comb from his pocket, and carefully combed his hair. Mom carried a large plate of scrambled eggs to the table and turned to the boy as he turned from the mirror. She reached out and messed up his hair, laughing, and said, "Aww, you didn't do that right!" He was surprised and stunned at the quick action, but quickly saw the humor and changed his expression. The don't-look-at-me face burst out with a laugh at her prank. He turned back to the mirror for a quick do-over before we sat down for breakfast. That act seemed to have broken a tense atmosphere.

In the free-time, Mom and the boys talked with each other. They all had scars of suffering and abuse. Mom understood, and she had a winning way with most of the boys. After the boys "graduated" from the home, many of them sent wedding invitations to Mom when they were getting married.

CHAPTER 15

A BEAUTIFUL SUNSET

Years later my dad's life seeped away slowly until he breathed his last. My sorrow was not in that he was gone but that he never apologized on his own free will. He never expressed regret for his actions or spoke words of affirmation or love to his wife or children. Mom was a widow but not sorrowful.

Through the hard times, we had learned to draw strength from God's Word, the Bible. The truth of the saying, "Adversity helps you become what you would never have been without it" became very true in my life.

About a year after Dad passed, I got a call from my sister. Mom was now living with her.

"Are you sitting down?" my sister began the phone call.

"I'm driving," I answered.

Then she asked, "What would you say if I told you Mom is writing letters back and forth with a man?"

I burst out laughing. This was so far from my mind; it struck me as funny. This was unbelievable! Mom would never…. Every time I tried to say something I could not speak because of laughter. I laughed and laughed. It was uncontrollable. I finally hung up. When I got home and got some control of the laughter, I called her back and got a little more of the details.

It was true. A kindly Amish gentleman was showing interest in my mom. None of the rest of us had known about this growing relationship. My sister got Mom's permission to let us know what was going on. Mom was doing a lot of laughing as well. There was a new spark in her. This was for real. It was hard to believe this could be possible. My mind was spinning. I was mentally reliving the past and now trying to picture some kind of future. I fully trusted Mom; she would not do anything stupid.

The next day as the news began to sink in and become a reality, I began to cry. I cried nearly as hard as I had laughed the day before. Each series of thoughts triggered a new flood of tears. It would not be easy for any of us. The following days were mixed with laughter and tears. The more we talked and the days turned to weeks, I began to sense this was God's will, just like Mom said she did.

I pictured Joseph in the Old Testament. His hard life eventually landed him in prison -- just like Mom had been figuratively. Both were innocent sufferers, yet just like Joseph ended up sitting beside the "highest in the land," so my mom would sit beside a well-known, highly respected Amish bishop and leader of many people. How could this be!

Mom was misunderstood by many. She had a sad face in those years, married to my dad. I'm sure many didn't know *what* to say. Many times, at the church gatherings, few spoke to her; sometimes no one spoke one word to her.

She always felt that people looked down on her, even blamed her. She now believes that people just didn't know what to say and that the whole situation made them uncomfortable.

News of this new budding relationship quickly spread far and wide in the Amish community. Many were happy for my mom. Many were surprised. Some unpleasantly surprised, "He is getting married to *WHO*?" someone said, "In the Bible days, folks would tear their clothes and sit in ashes dressed in sackcloth." If only that person had known the depth of despair and suffering that she had endured for so many hard years.

Those that got to know my mom liked her. Only a few knew her heart. Many of the youth liked her. She was a good cook and served up attractive and delicious meals. Mom dared to think outside-of-the-box. She was creative and clever. Often a new recipe was a marked winner!

The man that had an interest in her had been a very sad widower for around a year. My parents were acquainted with Monroe and his wife years earlier. His wife had died after a battle with cancer.

He struggled with the huge loss and cried every day. The loneliness felt like more than he could bear.

When Monroe's granddaughter married a boy from Mom's church, they met again for the first time after losing their spouses. It is traditional for everyone in the church to be invited to the wedding of one of the youth. Monroe's eyes scanned the eligible widows. He had been praying for a partner and asking God's guidance since his wife had died. He was so very sad and lonely, almost beside himself with grief. He was a people person and did not do well alone.

"Which one do You have for me, Lord?" Monroe prayed, "God, I'm so lonesome. Somewhere out there is a Christian widow my age. Someone who I can get along with and who gets along with me." He felt God would bring him a wife. He told me that when he saw my mom that morning, his heart quickened.

"Is this the one, Lord? If so, bring her to me." She made her way through the crowd that afternoon to say hello and to see if he remembered her. He was

talking to his children when she came up to him –
just as he had asked God to do in his prayer.

They shook hands. Monroe took her hand in
both of his, saying, "Lena!" At that moment the
electricity began. He was looking for a life partner;
Mom was not. In fact, when he asked her if she'd
ever consider marrying again, she said, "Absolutely
not! I will *never* let another man hurt me."

Just days before they got married, her five-
year-old granddaughter, who was very close to her
grandma said, "I wish that old man would just go
back home and leave us like we were."

We all liked "that old man," but like the
granddaughter, we realized things would be
different. He was on a mission. He would fetch his
wife, and she would be moving five hours away
from us. The granddaughter put into words
something that we were all feeling. But *our* ways are
often not God's way.

They got married four months after meeting
again at the granddaughter's wedding. When Mom
married Monroe, I realized that made a very big

family. He had thirteen children, and together with Mom's eleven, that made 24 of us!

After they were married, he took her to his home. They were so very happy together. It was a great healing for my mom. I was with some ladies from her home church, and the usual question came up, "How's your mom doing?"

"Well," I said, "I just heard about their first disagreement the other day," They looked surprised and wanted to hear this bit of news. "Seems they don't agree as to who got the better end of this deal!"

Who but Monroe could have taken her away like that, and she could still be happy? She enjoyed going places with him, and they traveled to several states and even out of the country. They were good companions and spent many happy hours talking.

Chapter 16

A FUNERAL

Monroe died Thursday, February 11, 2016. I packed as quickly as possible and drove the two hours to reach Mom who was eagerly waiting for at least one of us to be with her. They had lived in Worthington, Indiana for the first year of their marriage, but moved to Belle Center, Ohio which was three hours closer to our home.

Could it possibly be? He was gone! It was almost unbelievable.

In January, Monroe had a cold when they came home from their trip to Nicaragua where they spent their fifth wedding anniversary with my oldest brother. After their trip, they spent a few days at my sister Orpha's house. Orpha took him to urgent care and got him some medicine. He got over the cold and said he felt good again. That lasted a short time before he started feeling weak and tired again. He was not in the habit of making a beaten path to the doctor and didn't want to go now. He felt that he would get over it, he always had.

On that Thursday morning, he told Mom that he was ready to go to see a doctor. Mom didn't go along because she uses a walker and did not want to get in the way. Monroe's son David went with him.

The doctor said, "This is serious," and mentioned the possibility of blood clots. He wanted them to go to a hospital immediately.

Monroe used his driver's phone to call Mom and tell her the news. "This is going to be so hard for Lena," he told David with tears in his eyes.

The doctor was south of Monroe's home, and the hospital was north of it. Monroe was dropped off at his home, and he and Mom got ready while David went to his home and picked up his wife. Just minutes passed before David and Miriam were back.

After they were ready, Monroe went to sit where he could see them drive in. He wanted to be out the door and on his way without delay. Mom was at the sink finishing a final clean up. She didn't know when they would be back again. She had an urge to look in his direction and saw that his head was tipped over backward to the floor. There had been no sound. She hurried over to help him, calling, "Monroe, can you hear me?"

He didn't respond. His color had changed to bluish purple. She struggled to get his head lifted up on another chair. He was able to use his elbow to help boost himself into a sitting position. He could not talk. At this point, David and his wife came in. When they didn't see Monroe at the door they were concerned, and they both hurried inside. There was my mom, holding him in her arms.

David cried, "DAD! *DAD!*" but he was gone.

He died in her arms in the surroundings of their home. It was just as he would have chosen. They were alone, yet not for long. She didn't have to leave him to call for help. However sorry they were to let him go, they could see when looking back, it was much more peaceful this way than if they had made it to the hospital. His life was finished. No wires and machines were hooked up to him, no doctors and nurses hurrying around, shooing Mom away while they fixed things. No hospital bills.

The doctors figured that it was a blood clot which caused a heart attack. Everything had changed in such a short time. We all rejoice, knowing he is now where he longed to be. He often spoke of Heaven and his desire to go there. The day before his passing he discussed finances with Mom and the possibility of his going first. They often talked openly about dying and where they would prefer to be buried. His desire was to be buried in Worthington, Indiana, beside his first wife; though he let his children make that final decision.

The news spread quickly, and the Amish people in the community came together to help with the cleaning and with the preparations. The funeral and viewing were to be held in a large building that was built for this type of emergency, heatable and suitable for large crowds. It was normally used as a barn and machinery shed. The machinery had to be moved along with five to seven loads of hay. They used power washers to wash and clean the inside of the building. Because so many people showed up wanting to help, they even assigned some to clean out the horse barn and put down fresh straw. By late that evening, the preparations were finished.

On Friday, the viewing lasted for three hours with around 400 people coming through the line. On Saturday there was another four-hour viewing with a break in the middle. Again, around 400 people came. The funeral was on Sunday, Valentine's Day, with around a thousand people attending. The noon meal was served to all. Most of the people left before the evening meal, but 100 to 200 remained.

Three of Monroe's thirteen children live in Belle Center near where Mom and Monroe lived. Meals were brought in to each of their homes and to Mom's. They asked us if we wanted a hot breakfast casserole. We declined, but the noon and evening meals were brought in, served, and cleaned up. His children's homes had not only their children but their brothers and sisters who came from out-of-state with their families.

On Monday the trip was made to Indiana for the burial. Monroe's three children from Belle Center hired a driver with a van. Four of us plus Mom shared the cost of the trip and rode with them. We had a good time getting to know each other better. I enjoyed singing songs together with beautiful harmony.

As we traveled, some chips were passed around for a snack. The youngest son, Jerry, said that when they got into their buggy after the funeral, there was a grocery bag with several bags of chips. A note was attached saying, "For your trip Monday." Now *that* was a church reaching out and blessing those in mourning!

The days following the funeral were very difficult. Mom couldn't stay alone. She knew she would have to pack up and move back closer to her children. How she dreaded leaving this place where they had spent those few, short, wonderful years! How could she leave all this? She loved the church people and his family. It had become home, and this home was packed with fond, loving memories. What a healing experience God had allowed to happen!

Mom said that two days before Monroe died, she heard music. The next day she heard it again. "It was Heavenly music -- like nothing we hear around here," she said. Each time she heard it while she sat at her sewing machine. When she realized what she was hearing and focused on it, it was gone.

God knew she needed it. He cares when we cry and when we hurt. He knows how it feels when we cry. "Jesus wept" (John 11:35). He knows what it is to be forsaken. "Then all the disciples deserted him and fled" (Matthew 26:56b). He also knows exactly what we need. "And my God will meet all your needs according to the riches of his glory in Christ Jesus" (Philippians 4:19).

God knew just how hard it would be for Mom when Monroe was gone. We are in good hands when we give ourselves to Him. Now we look back and see the good work that God had done in the five years of their marriage. What will He do in the next five years? If we choose God and hear His voice and obey, I am confident He will work many marvelous things in all of our lives. "'For I know the plans I have for you,' declares the Lord, 'plans to prosper you and not to harm you, plans to give you hope and a future'" (Jeremiah 29:11).

"Were you ever angry with God for taking him?" I asked Mom one day.

"No, never. I know God doesn't make mistakes," she answered. "I can handle the grief of loss better when I think of him in Heaven now, gone to his reward. He is finished here. God has allowed me to see him in dreams. Always, in my dreams, he is happy. I saw him looking at me with his loving eyes. I saw his kind face and heard his voice," her voice broke as she spoke, "which I miss so-o-o much!"

CHAPTER 17

AWAY FROM THE FENCE

Writing my story has taken me back to memories, many of which I never wanted to revisit. I carry scars of degrading verbal abuse from my father, but God's Word is my constant source of life and healing. God's promises are like ointment to the old scars and wounds. He brings me hope, strength, and newness as I walk in the path that He has for me. I had a thought while writing this book, *God has books too*. In Psalm 139:16 it says, "Your eyes saw my unformed body; all the days ordained for me were written in your book before one of them came to be." I was in God's mind, plans, and intentions before I was formed. How intricate, great, and wonderful our God and Creator is!

One way that God helped me to see what He had for my path came in a vision that I had soon after we returned from our trip to Canada. I was by myself in familiar surroundings, life as I knew it. There were trees, the barn, and other comfortable things surrounding me. One of the things was a strong, board fence. Suddenly, everything changed, and I was standing alone in the same spot, but now it was an open field. Everything around me was gone. I felt so vulnerable.

"Lord," I cried in amazed desperation, "What will I do when the storms come?" All that surrounded me was tall grass, gently moving in the breeze.

"Am I not enough?" He spoke those words to my spirit. I knew that He was showing me that I must let go of everything that I had trusted and totally lean on Him to be my protection; His Word would be my guide.

I am often asked, "What was the hardest part of leaving?" It was the rejection of our people. The condemnation weighed heavily on us. Driving our car past the homes of our Amish friends for the first time was not easy. Knowing that in their eyes we were on our way to Hell for leaving God, the church, and their rules. But we hadn't left God. We had left everything to fully lean and trust in Him. In time, God replaced our friends that we lost from the Amish church with many more dear friends.

Another adjustment was the change in our way of dressing. The outward appearance was our important focus for all those years, and now it was okay to dress differently. Many used clothes were given to us which was a blessing because we couldn't afford new, but all my life I had one style or pattern for my dress. Now with all the choices, I didn't know what matched or what was appropriate attire to wear to which events. I didn't know what was "in" or who figured out what "in" was, and why it was "in"!

For a long time after I left the Amish church, I still wore a head covering. It set me apart. I didn't feel Amish or English. The reasoning for wearing a headcovering comes from I Corinthians 11. I became convinced that it was a custom and that our new church "had no such custom" (v. 16). It became more clear to me one day that it was a custom when I went to shop at a bulk food store in "Amish Country" after I had quit wearing a head covering. Because I still felt condemned by some of the Amish people, the people-pleasing side of me decided to wear a loose hanging cloth on my head. Head coverings are usually black or white, but I chose tan. People asked me where I was from and what church I belonged to. I knew that the questions came because of my covering and long dress. Because of the symbol on my head, they wondered what "flavor" I belonged to. That was the last time that I tried to please people by wearing a headcovering. I had experienced the covering as a label of which "flavor" I was. I was none of them, and I do not want to be labeled as one.

One aspect that has been hard to deal with in the English world is the differences in child training. Many parents in the English world don't seem to expect much from their children, and that is what they get -- not much. I was used to expected obedience such as children sitting quietly with their parents in church for three hours on hard wooden benches without backs. If a child was told to come, they came. It bothers me when a toddler is told to come and instead of coming, he takes off running. I think that it is bad when the parent chases after them, or even worse, when they think that it is "cute."

There are some things that I still do, like hanging my laundry out to dry. I have a dryer, but I don't use it much. I made our bread when the children were home, and I still make granola and "Grape Nuts" for our own use. We heat with wood, and I have a wood stove in the kitchen which is our main source of heat in the winter. I cook on it in the wintertime too. I don't turn on lights as quickly as many do. I still have a garden every year, and I work in it barefooted. Later, I can my good, fresh garden vegetables.

In my Amish life, the implication was that because I was Amish, I was God's accepted child and on my way to Heaven. In my Amish life, we spoke of *us* (Amish) and *them* (the world). It was implied that if we were a good and obedient follower of the rules of the *Ordnung,* then God was pleased.

There are some things about the Amish life which make it a nice way to live, yet there was something missing in my life. It seemed that God was a silent God. In the beginning, He spoke, and there was light. He spoke to Moses, Abraham, David, and so many of His servants a long time ago. I had learned about these men and many more. I knew that God was good, He loved His people, and that He was supreme. I am so grateful that I learned these things about God at a young age, but in my Amish life it felt like God was a distant, powerful figure of the past. It left me wondering where He was in my life today. Could I reach or hear Him? I wanted a daily, living, relationship with God in my life. I wanted God to be first in my decision-making, thoughts, and actions.

The pain in my life put me on a journey to find God in a deeper way. The rules and traditions came up empty and had nothing to offer when my heart was breaking. Just being Amish did not qualify me for entrance into Heaven. My good works did not qualify me for entrance into Heaven. I could depend on NOTHING but the pure and precious blood of Jesus for my salvation. By His sacrifice of death on the cross, He paid my sin debt. I have received that gift. He is my Lord and Savior. The works that I do are in *response* to what He has done for me. "We love Him because He first loved us" (1 John 4:19). What I do can not earn my entrance into Heaven. It is a free gift.

God became the sure and trusted foundation in my life. I discovered that He is the only one that can fill the emptiness inside. He is the missing part that many are seeking. Many struggle through life trying to find fulfilment with things that money can buy. They think, "When I get this, or accomplish that, I'll be happy." Nothing, oh reader, can fill that place but God. He has a plan and a purpose for each created human being and can turn our messed up lives into beauty.

71641035R00102

Made in the USA
Middletown, DE
26 April 2018